HIGHLIGHTS FROM

DAVE MATTHEWS
TIM REYNOLDS

LIVE AT LUTHER COLLEGE

D0127563

Transcribed by Jeff Jacobson and Paul Pappas
Back cover photo by Sam Erickson
Inside photography © Jay Blakesberg

ISBN 1-57560-275-X

Visit our website at www.cherrylane.com

BAND IN A BOX

BACKSTAGE WITH ACOUSTIC ROCK MAVERICKS

DAVE MATTHEWS AND TIM REYNOLDS

BY JEFFREY PEPPER RODGERS

On this crisp spring afternoon outside the Berkeley Community Theater, there's no mistaking the preparations for the ritual called the Big Rock Show. Roadies are unloading a truckful of gear through the closely guarded stage door, and teen and college-age fans—some of whom have traveled from several states away—are milling around, hoping for a glance, an autograph, or a photo op with the Big Rock Star known as Dave Matthews.

Inside the theater, though, any suggestion of a hyped-up "show" vanishes. On the stage sit only five acoustic guitars, a chair, and a few mics, boxes, and cords. The crew is casual but focused, and when Matthews arrives, he greets everyone with a familial friendliness. With his short hair, athletic frame, cotton sweater, and khakis, he looks less like a rock star than a fraternity brother from up the hill at the University of California. His duo partner, Tim Reynolds, makes quite a contrast – short, wiry, and a bit scraggly, all in black from punker boots on up, he's ready for underground clubbing.

The show tonight marks the end of Matthews' and Reynolds' latest acoustic tour, following the release of their double CD *Live at Luther College,* recorded in 1996. With two acoustic guitars and Matthews'

alternately wailing/whispering voice, this duo brings to life the knotty, intense songs that have made the Dave Matthews Band such a compelling and surprising force in contemporary rock. The DMB is emphatically a band, democratically balancing acoustic guitar, sax, violin, drums, and bass (the sole electric instrument) in expansive arrangements full of harmonic and rhythmic jags. But it's amazing how much of that richness and variety comes across in these duo shows. It's a testimony to the depth of Matthews' vision as a songwriter and guitarist, and to Reynolds' range as an accompanist, from subtle doubling to delay-based atmospherics to pure shredding.

As Matthews and Reynolds grab guitars and sit down with me to talk and play music, it's immediately clear that despite their surface differences, these are very close friends and partners in crime. Reynolds has played on all the DMB albums and frequently joins the band on stage, in addition to pursuing his own projects in freewheeling solo guitar improv, rock, and funk. In conversation, Reynolds and Matthews feed off each other's kinetic energy and quick humor (sly and urbane one moment, locker-room adolescent the next), and when Matthews starts playing something on guitar, Reynolds locks in with him in a microbeat.

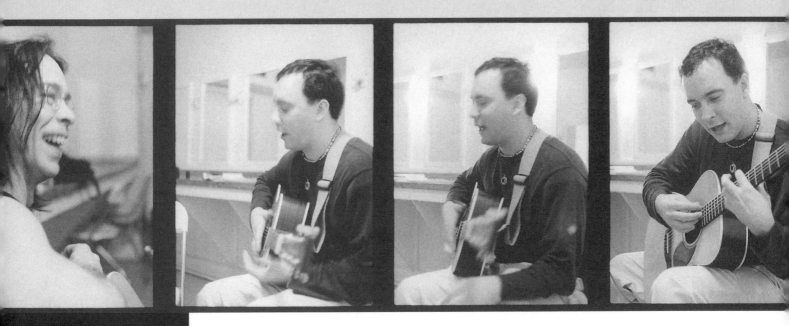

I've heard that you two met when Tim was playing in a bar in Charlottesville, Virginia, and Dave was the bartender. Is that a true story?

MATTHEWS Mmm, sort of. I think we met before I started working at Millers. We lived in the same town, and I love watching music, and Tim was one of the Charlottesville musicians –

REYNOLDS – posers.

MATTHEWS Posers. I just loved Tim's playing, so then we just got to know each other. The cool thing was that people like Tim had [the trio] TR3, he was doing his solo thing, he was playing jazz gigs, he had tons of gigs. All the musicians were sort of wrapped up together. Carter [Beauford], who's with [the Matthews Band] on drums, played in Secrets and Tim was playing in Secrets, and they probably crossed paths in a lot of different situations.

And two of the guys who sat in on this last album [*Before These Crowded Streets*] were also old friends of ours from Charlottesville – Greg Howard [Chapman Stick] and John D'earth [string arrangements].

Tim, were you playing free-improv acoustic guitar at that time?

REYNOLDS At that point I was probably doing electric, but that evolved. I did that gig for over ten years. It started out solo electric guitar with effects, and somewhere I started playing sitar and did that for a long time, and then I started playing acoustic.

MATTHEWS Monday night at Millers . . . I remember coming in, it was electric for a while, and then all of a sudden violin, and then all of a sudden cello, and then sitar. And then he'd even play drums for a while–it was cool.

REYNOLDS I learned to play a lot of instruments on this gig. And that kind of led to the acoustic guitar as encom-passing all the earlier stuff. I got way into that with the effects.

MATTHEWS And then he'd play a lot of Eastern-sounding scales and weird drums on the guitar.

When you first started playing together, were you doing Dave's songs?

MATTHEWS Not really, not for a while. We started recording stuff in my basement or over at his house. I remember Joseph, his son, playing the drums with the balls on the end of the sticks. We'd do some silly recordings. It was open because we hadn't yet been defined.

We had fun together, and then I, sort of at the [suggestion] of Tim and a few other people, started the Matthews Band. A couple of songs had been written before the band, but we worked them up and started playing them. And it was only really after that that Tim and I got together and started playing acoustically. Remember we did the Prism [coffeehouse] thing? That was the first time the two of us played two acoustics together.

Tim was also involved in the band's first album. Dave, what were you looking for him to bring into those sessions?

MATTHEWS Tim and I had been playing acoustic gigs, and it just made sense to bring Tim in, to have some of that spirit, the vibe we had together.

Tim, did you play more acoustic or electric on the early band albums?

REYNOLDS A lot of acoustic. I'd spend about two months playing acoustic and three days playing electric.

MATTHEWS It was us sitting next to each other, strumming madly. It was so much fun.

REYNOLDS We sat in the studio just like this [*moves chair right in front of Matthews*] with a glass thing [between us], and that's how we did the whole first record. The band was all on the second floor.

MATTHEWS And then they'd inevitably turn his acoustic guitar way up and mine way down! That's [producer Steve] Lillywhite–I'm not saying whether he was right or wrong, but he'd say [*affects British accent*], "OK, let's turn David down and Timmy up" [*laughs*]. I love how with the last album, he said, "David, you don't really feature on this album at all, but don't tell anyone." We'd learn it, we'd all play, and then he'd turn me down.

Were you playing the same parts?

REYNOLDS On the first album we played the same part and then doubled it – like four acoustic guitars playing the same thing.

MATTHEWS And it made it sound really huge.

REYNOLDS I would just overdub a little bit. I did more electric overdubs as the albums went on.

MATTHEWS The last one has a lot more production. We still recorded the rhythm section live – guitar, bass, and drums – but then much more stuff went on top. Oh, put Stick there, piano . . . it doesn't matter if they're not in the band. We had a lot of other people. And Tim taped his face up and played lots of electric overdubs [*laughs*].

Dave, have you always played exclusively acoustic?

MATTHEWS I never really played electric. Sometimes when I pick one up, I'm surprised. It's amazing how suddenly you're just like [makes wailing rock lead sounds]. Yeah, I know what that feels like now! And then I put it down, and I just sit back down with an acoustic.

What drew you to playing an acoustic in the first place?

MATTHEWS I think in the first place it was a percussive thing. Also it's lighter and there are less things you need with it, so when I was younger and just traveling around, doing a lot of walking, it was always easier to have an acoustic. So I sort of grew attached to how portable it was. And when you're 16 and you can play "Father and Son" by Cat Stevens, [sings] "It's not time to make a change . . ." all of a sudden you're making out.

It's interesting that you've always played an acoustic, because you hardly ever play standard acoustic guitar open-position chords. Instead, you favor closed positions and up-the-neck things that are more typical of electric playing. How did that style evolve?

MATTHEWS I think one of the biggest inspirations was John D'earth. He's a trumpet player and a great teacher as well; he did the string arrangements on the last album. But he once said to me, "Guitarists always write everything in E or A or D." So I started playing as many things as I could that were a half step away.

Do you come up with those closed-position patterns by hunting and pecking?

MATTHEWS A lot of things that I do come out of trying to find circular motions. I'll just go around and around with something–unlike Tim. I think one reason we're complementary is that I can play the same five notes in the same order for an hour and find it absolutely satisfying. And Tim can swim around; I don't know if Tim ever repeats himself. So then the two of us kind of land comfortably together.

One of your signature guitar parts is the staccato "Satellite" riff, which opens up a lot of possibilities for Tim to play more sustained or legato types of things. It's not like playing over a big strum.

DAVE MATTHEWS' RHYTHM STYLE

Like Richard Thompson, Ani DiFranco, and other top songwriter-guitarists, Dave Matthews has developed a potent and highly individual guitar style that is inextricably linked to his songwriting. He sticks to standard tuning, with an occasional sixth-string drop to D, but uses a chord vocabulary that is anything but standard. During the course of our interview, Matthews demonstrated the rhythm parts from numerous songs, and some clear stylistic patterns emerged.

First, Matthews is far less bound by open strings than most acoustic players, which is one reason why he never uses a capo. He's as comfortable playing in a key like Ab ("Satellite"), without using even a single open string, as in the usual E, G, A, and D. The same goes for his drone-oriented parts. While "Minarets," for example, is in the open-string–friendly key of E (played up in seventh position to get octave E's on the fifth and sixth strings), he plays an equally driving drone in "Warehouse" in the key of B (also up in seventh position) with no open strings. Even when he tunes to dropped-D, it isn't necessarily for playing in the key of D; in "Crush," he tunes down but plays in Bm and never hits the sixth string open in the entire song. So why retune? To facilitate off-the-beaten-track fingerings.

Matthews' preference for closed chords means, of course, using plenty of barre chords, often reduced to two- and three-note modal voicings (without the third, neither major nor minor). Watching him navigate through numerous progressions, I was struck by how economical his parts are; typically, he goes to one position and stays put, making whatever stretches are necessary to reach the notes rather than moving around the neck. "Satellite" is a case in point: the main riff is a little circle of notes played on the bottom three strings while his index finger stays planted at the fourth fret.

By steering away from garden-variety open chords and keys, Matthews sets his songs apart from most guitar-based music right from the downbeat. There are other advantages to this style: Closed positions allow more control over string percussion, which he uses heavily, particularly in the duo with Reynolds. And when Matthews does opt for an open chord, it makes a dramatic contrast – an instant lift for a chorus or a bridge.

REYNOLDS Yeah, exactly. It's clearly different, especially where there are just two guitars. With a band you can come up with a really simple part, because everyone else is laying down a lot of other stuff. But with two acoustic guitars, you have to be more aware of [the other guitar part].

Tim, do you come up with the guitar melodies you play in "Satellite" and other songs when you're jamming?

REYNOLDS I just come up with it in the studio, and Steve, the producer, says, "Stick with that." And that becomes the theme. It becomes part of the song.

MATTHEWS It really does. And people get excited when they hear that. When the band is live and Tim is not with us, I don't think people generally miss things, but people definitely react [when they hear that guitar line]. With "Crash," when they hear the little signature things that Timmy does, the pull-offs and stuff, they go "Yaaaah!" It's almost more familiar than everything else.

REYNOLDS The [duo] thing is like a band. Because we play with bands, we hear a lot more in our heads than what we play. The psychic vibe of a band comes in, and we just lock in like a band.

MATTHEWS Sometimes I'm amazed by how it locks in, really amazed.

There are a lot of songs on the live record with intense drone parts. I'm thinking, for instance, of "Warehouse."

REYNOLDS Oh yeah, I tune this down [*tunes sixth string down to B*]. And then I have this pedal that in the backward mode can make it go up an octave or down. I set it so that it will go down. So I get this drone going and repeat it and then I make it go down an octave. You can't get too busy with the backwards mode – it starts to pile up. But the chip lets it bleed off naturally, so we turn it off and just stop. You can do a lot of stuff where you play one thing and then it'll repeat a couple of times and you can actually play your next part, so there are two, three things going on at once just for a minute.

MATTHEWS That definitely gets into a nice wall. So by the time we get into the body of the song, when it sucks back, this little window opens.

Tim, do you ever feel limited when you're using effects with an acoustic guitar?

REYNOLDS No, it's the opposite. I play so much electric guitar that I get my ya-yas out with that, and when I'm playing acoustic, I don't ever feel I need that. I get off on doing both.

I can play acoustic guitar without effects–I practice that way, and I've made records without them, but I like to have more colors. I have lots of records of acoustic guitars, but I don't listen

"I get inspired by Tim a lot, but it's also a place that I haven't gone to..."

to them as much as I listen to other records that have a lot more sounds. But that's just my own taste, and my tastes always change, so that's only today.

"Minarets," "The Last Stop," and other songs make heavy use of Middle Eastern–sounding scales.

REYNOLDS Yeah. I used to like bebop because it had a zillion chords, but then I kind of overloaded on that concept and got into Eastern music, which is just one chord, and I could relate to John Lee Hooker again. And that opened up a whole different way of improvising, based on sound as opposed to notes, and then mixing them together again. You know, you can play just one note forever [*plays note with slow, watery bend*]. You're just messing around there instead of like [*plays fast bop-style lines*]– the nervous Western industrial society approach. Am I penis yet? [*laughter*] For hyper people like me, that's a great energy.

MATTHEWS But then Tim can access both of those.

REYNOLDS John McLaughlin is known for going ape shit, right? But with Shakti, he does these beautiful opening bits, the Indian approach. He does these beautiful bends, Ravi Shankar kind of stuff where he bends it so much you can hear him tune the guitar back up during the song.

Dave, what inspired you to explore Eastern territory in your songwriting?

MATTHEWS I get inspired by Tim a lot, but it's also a place that I haven't gone to and have always loved. If you're playing something like [*plays rhythmic drone on two strings*], eventually, if you don't like it, you're not listening [*laughs*]. And then after a while, when you go [*drops drone down one step*] or just a tiny change, it makes it so dramatic.

REYNOLDS With Steve Lillywhite, any time you do any Eastern thing, he goes, "Oh, it's Adrian Belew." Because that's his only reference point for anything like that. You're doing a deep raga and he goes, "Oh, it's Adrian Belew." It's like, "Steve, take your rich ass over to India for a while" [*laughter*].

Dave's songs start with his guitar but take on a different identity when the band arranges

them. Is it hard to go back and play them with two guitars and forget about what all the other instruments were doing?

MATTHEWS It's easy to forget about everything else that was going on. Some songs are a bit of a challenge–there are certain songs that we haven't even tried. "Crush" was one that I didn't know if it would work out. For some reason, in the studio [with the band] that song was a struggle. Finally we just said, "Well, let's just play it real straight." Then Fonzi [bassist Stefan Lessard] found this groove that was like Marvin Gaye, and we were like, "Oh, that's good." And so the song fell in there when the Marvin Gaye came out, at least in the bass.

I just never thought of this song after that as being something that would work without that feel, and it was a really pleasant surprise when Tim and I played it. It was just [*snaps fingers*]. It's really natural. It doesn't sound forced.

When you're playing with just two guitars, do you find that you play more percussively?

MATTHEWS Yeah. It doesn't come out as much with a band, you know. If I were using one of these [full-body acoustic] guitars, I don't know if it would work. I use a Chet Atkins because it's like [*makes sharp sound*].

REYNOLDS It's hard for an acoustic to cut through with all the instruments.

MATTHEWS Exactly. That's why it's so amazing when rock bands use acoustic guitars where it's like [*strums open A-minor chord; stops and makes wretching sound*]. Stop that, please, Bob!

A lot of times a part like that becomes just a little texture, especially if you throw an electric guitar on top of it. In your band arrangements, you manage to avoid that trap, even though there's a lot going on. Your guitar has its place.

MATTHEWS Yes. But I guess it's also the fact that there isn't an electric guitar all the time. It's not based around that. When we're doing albums or when Tim is playing with the band, it adds, but not everything is built around screaming rock guitar. There's a little more space.

WHAT THEY PLAY

The Dave Matthews and Tim Reynolds acoustic tour crew arrives with a truckload of road cases, but it's almost entirely PA and recording gear; the actual stuff used on stage would fit easily into the back of a Honda. At sound check, Matthews' longtime friend and guitar tech Monk Montgomery even apologizes about the simplicity of the stage setup as he walks me through it.

Reynolds plays two Martin D-35s, a '96 and a '93. Both have Martin's standard Fishman pickups, which run into a Morley volume pedal, a Boss digital delay, and then a Countryman direct box. The little Boss stomp box is the source of all of Reynolds' electronic trickery. "There's one backwards mode – it plays infinite, and you can mess with that," Reynolds says. "And there are delay modes that you can go infinite. There are a lot of cool little things."

For these duo shows, Matthews' main ax is a Martin HD-28, also Fishman equipped (the Gold Plus Natural 2) and running straight into a Countryman DI. "Even on the big tours we use Fishman," Montgomery says, "because it's really bright, and the way he plays so hard and a lot of low notes, it's the only thing that really captures the sound." Both Matthews' and Reynolds' guitars are miked (with a B&K 4051-A and an Audio-Technica 4021, respectively), but the signal only goes onto the night's board tape, not to the house. The Matthews crew (as well as fans) are inveterate tapers, and their archives are the source of releases like *Live at Luther College* and the DMB's *Live at Red Rocks.*

Matthews' backup six-string is a Lakewood M-32, which has its own integrated AER pickup system. And for a handful of songs–"Wild Horses," "Spoon," and "The Last Stop" –he picks up a Martin D12-28 12-string. (For "The Last Stop," it's tuned down a half step.)

All these guitars are strung with D'Addario lights. No funky tunings, and no capos or other gizmos except for Reynolds' slide. "Sorry, that's it," Montgomery says with a shrug. "I sit in that chair all night."

For band tours, Matthews has long been playing a Gibson Chet Atkins model that has been modified with Fishman electronics and runs through API preamps, Meyer CP-10 EQs, ⁣ ⁣ ⁣ide harmonizers. The Chet's thin, feedback-free ⁣ ⁣ ⁣s says, helps to cut through the dense band mix.

How much arranging do you do for playing as a duo?

REYNOLDS We know these songs almost in the way that someone who's played standards for years plays those songs every night, and can go anywhere with them. In a second you can tell this is the bridge. . . . It's almost like the music plays *us,* we play it so much. And when you play them that much, you don't give them life if you play them by rote; they have to change every night.

MATTHEWS I'm impressed when I see bands that just come out and do a note-for-note thing of their album, which is really like classical music. I'm impressed by that, because it must be *hard*. I would go out of my tree.

REYNOLDS When I was in Secrets, it was a great fusion band and there was a lot of improvising, but 99 percent of the time was all this synchronized tight shit. And that can get really boring fast, 'cause I like to improvise. I realized then that I wasn't cut out to be a fusion guy or anything like that. I had to be much looser.

[Dave's] songs give you an emotional thing, to open different chakras. It's real music, like all the ragas have a different meaning and emotion, and his songs cover all those colors.

How would you compare the whole experience of performing with the band versus the duo?

MATTHEWS I love playing with the band. I really, really love it. But there are more personalities, obviously... There's still the joy, there's still the generosity, but it's more like there's a choreography about it. You have to be more aware of each other, and there's sometimes the threat of falling a little too much into habit.

With Tim, though, it's so intimate, it's like going out for a candlelit dinner, except we're not eating. And I also feel that to a certain degree, if I was to suddenly go [*makes jibberish noises*], in this environment, Tim would probably laugh. I don't know if it would be an appropriate thing to do with the band. There's a certain looseness about when the two of us are playing that's really beautiful and really different from the band. I feel like this is real precious, you know. The band, I'm amazed how quiet we can get, but Tim and I can get [*whispers*] real quiet.

How about from your side, Tim?

REYNOLDS Different layers of it are different. In the upper layers, you're playing a different instrument, different size crowds. Acoustic has more subtle things because there's no rhythm section, so you're not competing with more sound. Yet when you have a rhythm section, that allows you a different kind of melodic freedom.

So it's different but it's the same, because the more you get down to the ground layer of where it comes from, *we're* being played. Music is playing *us,* and we let it go the way it should go. Even if it's just for a second, that second lasts a long time. Whatever creates that is really the ultimate.

Unlike a lot of people who perform with rock bands, who get sort of timid when they unplug, all the intensity and dynamics are there in your acoustic show.

MATTHEWS I know exactly what you mean, when you go out and watch a band unplugged – especially if they try to bust out some mean electric licks. And it's like, "Don't do any of these, unless it's in humor – the acoustic will not be an electric guitar for you."

REYNOLDS And then someone like John Hammond can *rock* on an acoustic. It's amazing.

Some of the covers that you do are surprising, like John Prine's "Angel from Montgomery."

MATTHEWS I'd love to do Bonnie Raitt's version of that. We did a Marilyn Manson song last year ["Cryptorchid"]. We turned it into a beautiful song. It was great to play this lovely, sorrow-filled ballad about the arrival of bitterness and sadness and suicidal tendencies; I'd sing it, and then afterwards say, "That's a tune by Marilyn Manson" [*laughs*].

In your set, it's interesting to hear a song like "Angel from Montgomery," which has a standard folk/country chord progression, next to your songs, which almost never have standard progressions.

MATTHEWS But I love it in other people's tunes. I don't know why I can't write like that. I love tunes like "Wild Horses" or [Lyle Lovett's] "Boat"–what a great song. I can't do it like him – he's got such a great delivery.

When I listen to your songs for the first time, the parts almost always go somewhere other than where I think they're going to go.

MATTHEWS Maybe a lot of that comes from a

blatant lack of knowledge. In some ways, I'm freed up by the fact that I don't write –

REYNOLDS – that you haven't had chord progressions shoved down your throat, so you have a different way of looking at them. That's the shit, though, that's what makes it different. That's why most people, after they've learned everything, spend [so much time] unlearning. That's why when I used to play jazz, and I would write songs, I would never write a jazz song, because it would sound like jazz. I always liked it when it was something like an accident. Like John Lee Hooker talks about, "I never do my changes on the four or the eight, because that's what people expect of me. I don't even know what I'm going to do–I just do it the way I like it."

I think of the typical verse/chorus/bridge structure of a song as a little wheel that keeps turning at a predictable speed. Your songs are more expansive than that; their structure is less obvious.

MATTHEWS With some songs, I think about the sections forwards and backwards–like maybe here's the main body of the song, and then there's a sort of chorus, and then the main body of the song, then I'll do the sort of chorus again, but maybe I'll do it twice as long, then I'll have another chorus, then

"Music is math without the formulas —"

the next one I'll do twice as long. I think of a lot of it in math – not clearly in math, but like, "Well, that makes sense. That's balanced."

REYNOLDS Music is math without the formulas –

MATTHEWS – without the problem of ascribing. And then I write a lot in patterns. Like "Satellite" I started off as this [*plays dissonant fingering exercise*]. And we sometimes do that [in concert] – that's fun. It's amazing, people recognize it. And then when they're convinced it's the wrong song, we play it the right way.

That song sounds a lot more sinister that way. It's like the satellite that they've lost track of over at mission control.

MATTHEWS The one that's fucking up all the telephones! That's the one I'm voting for.

SELECTED DISCOGRAPHY

DAVE MATTHEWS AND TIM REYNOLDS

Live at Luther College, Bama Rags/RCA 67755 (1999).

DAVE MATTHEWS BAND

Before These Crowded Streets, RCA 67660 (1998).

Live at Red Rocks 8.15.95, Bama Rags/RCA 67587 (1997).

Crash, RCA 66904 (1996).

Under the Table and Dreaming, RCA 66449 (1994).

Recently (five-song EP), Bama Rags 2 (1994). Bama *Rags,* LLC, PO

Box 1911, Charlottesville, VA 22903; (804) 971-4829;

www.dmband.com.

Remember Two Things, Bama Rags 1 (1993).

TIM REYNOLDS

Tim Reynolds Live: Puke Matrix Tour, TR Music (1999). Electric trio

set. Available through www.timreynolds.com or Bama Rags (see above).

Gossip of the Neurons, TR Music (1996). Solo acoustic-electric guitar

improv, recorded live at Millers.

WEB

The Dave Matthews and Tim Reynolds Web Site,

www.geocities.com/Sunset Strip/Venue/9634. This fan site's offerings

include set lists, live photos, and a guitar tab archive.

ONE SWEET WORLD

Words and Music by
David J. Matthews

*2nd time, play w/slight variations ad lib till Bridge.

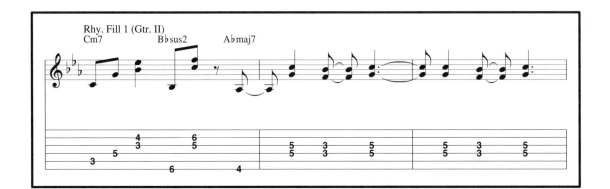

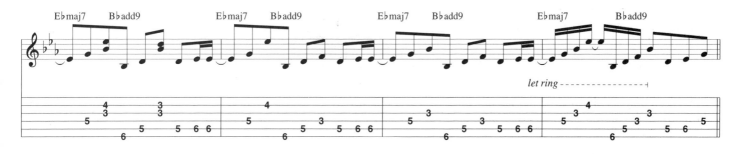

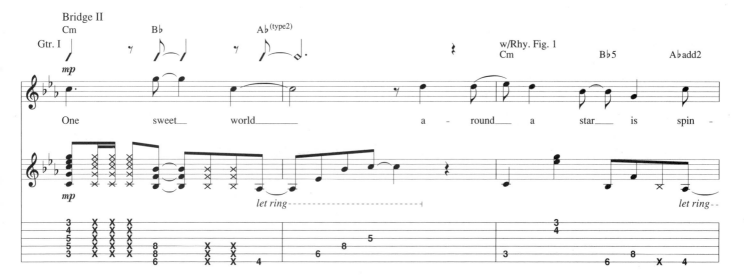

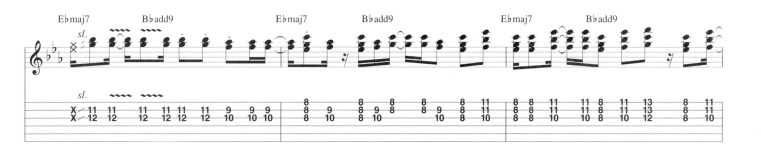

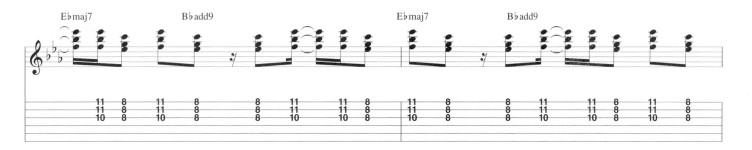

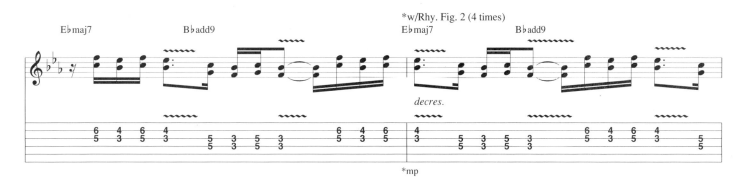

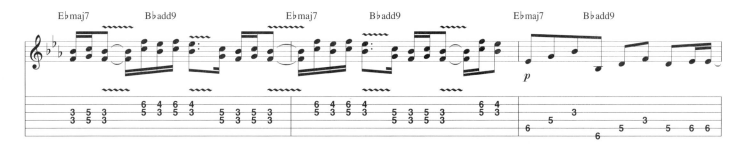

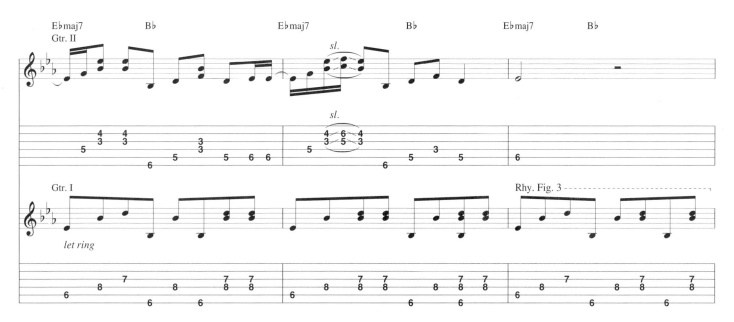

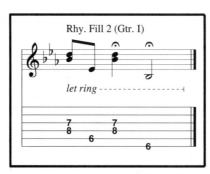

Additional Lyrics

2. If green should turn to grey,
   Would our hearts still bloody be?
   And if the mountains tumble away, the river dry,
   Would it stop the stepping feet? Oh...*(To Chorus)*

SATELLITE

Words and Music by
David J. Matthews

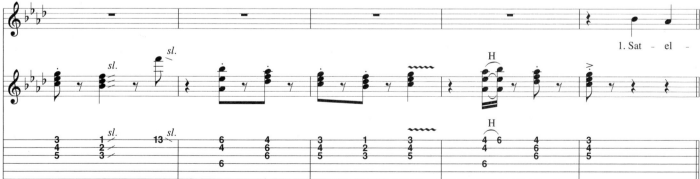

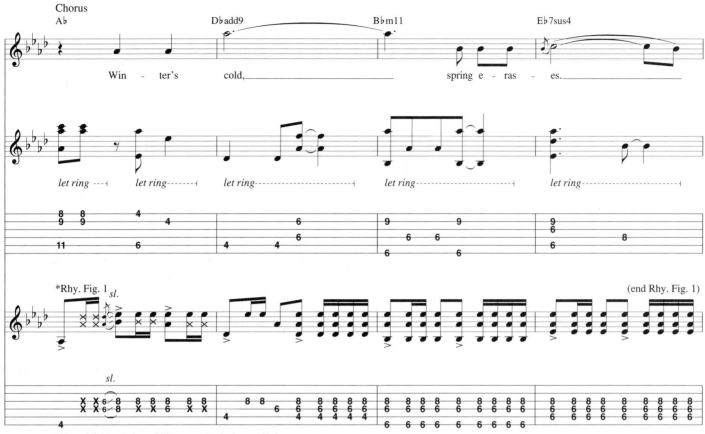

*Play w/slight variations ad lib on repeat and when recalled.

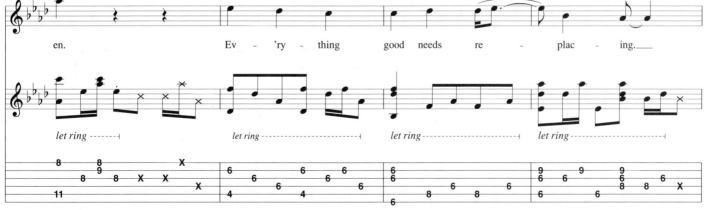

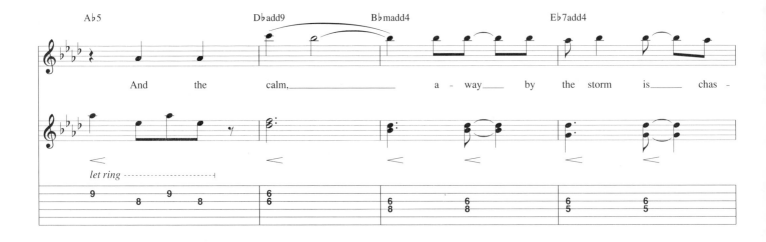

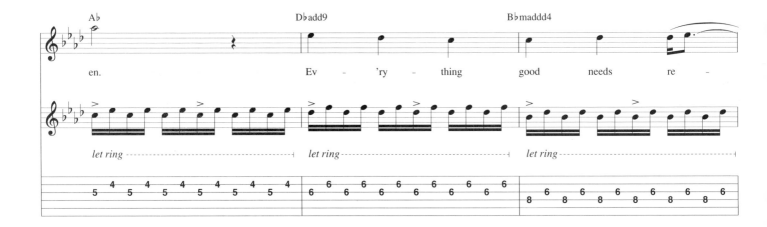

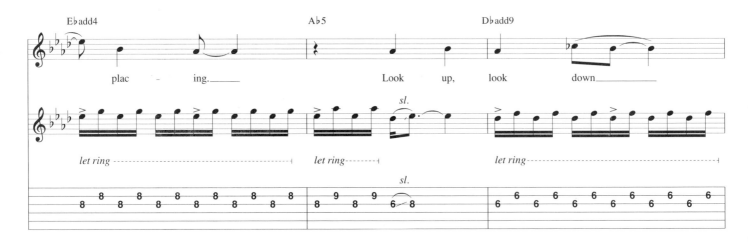

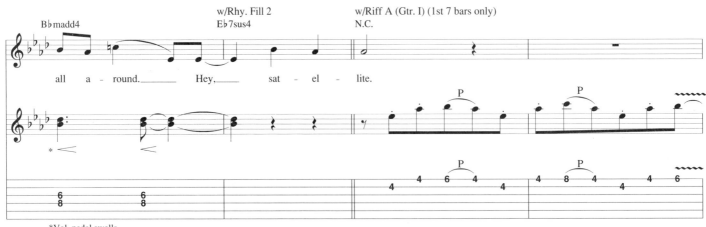

*Vol. pedal swells.

CRASH INTO ME

Words and Music by
David J. Matthews

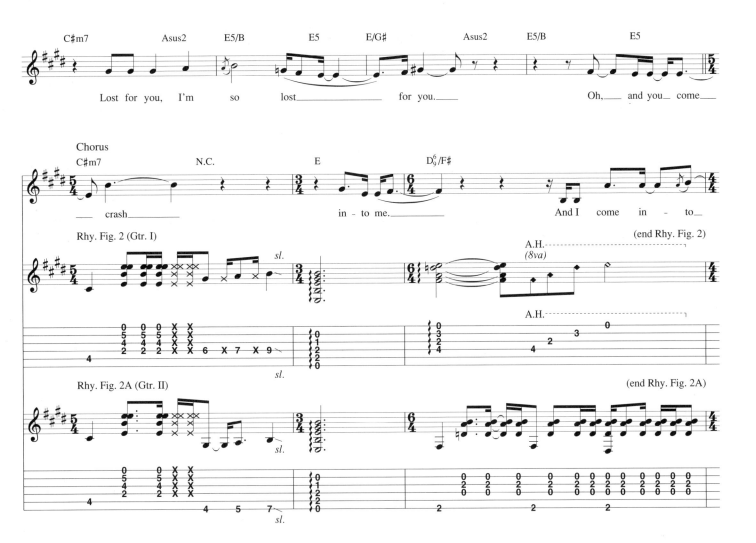

Lost for you, I'm so lost_____ for you._____ Oh,____ and you__ come____

Chorus

___ crash_____ in - to me._____ And I come in - to__

Rhy. Fig. 2 (Gtr. I)

Rhy. Fig. 2A (Gtr. II)

w/Rhy. Fig. 1 (Gtr. II) (2 times)

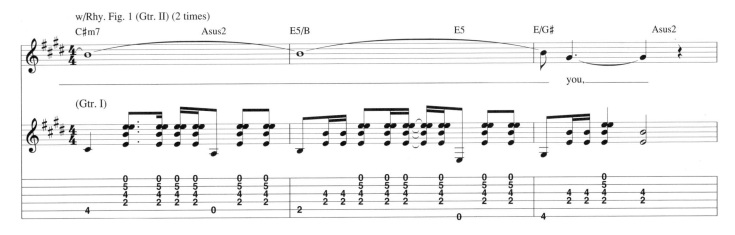

you,_____

(Gtr. I)

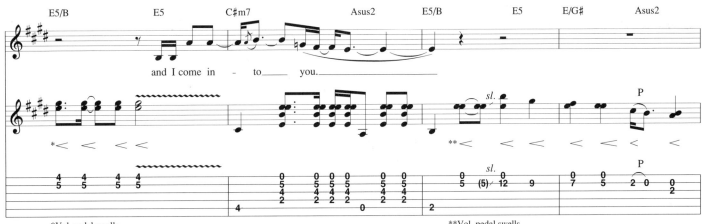

and I come in - to____ you.

*Vol. pedal swells.   **Vol. pedal swells.

29

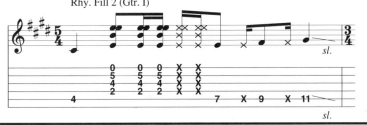

Outro
w/Rhy. Fig. 1 (Gtr. II) 6 times

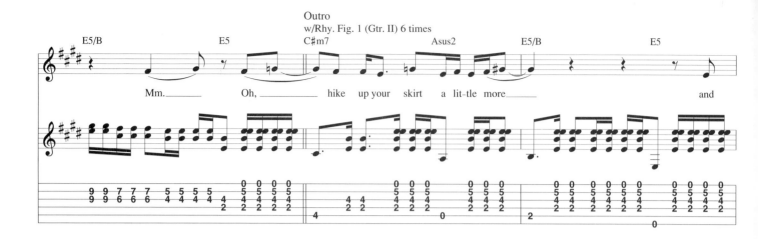

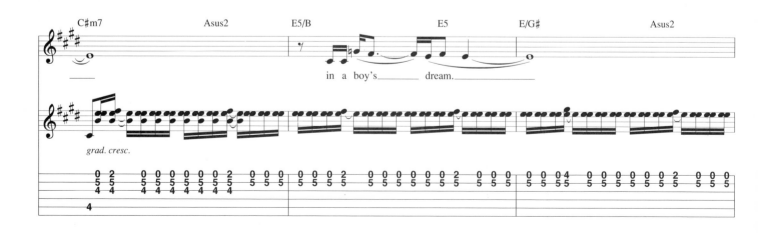

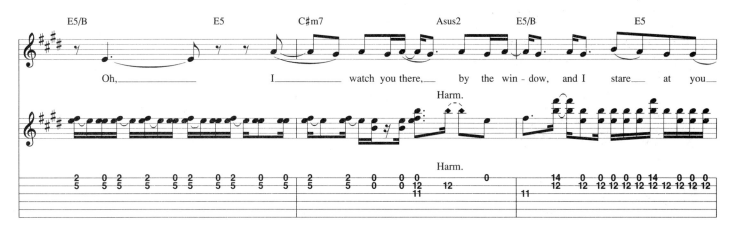

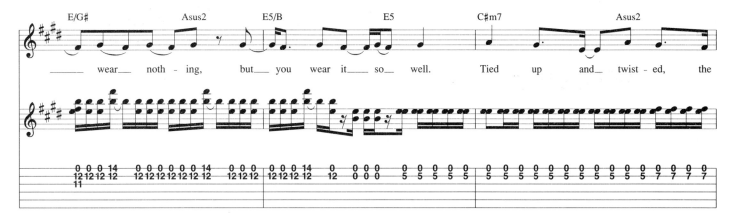

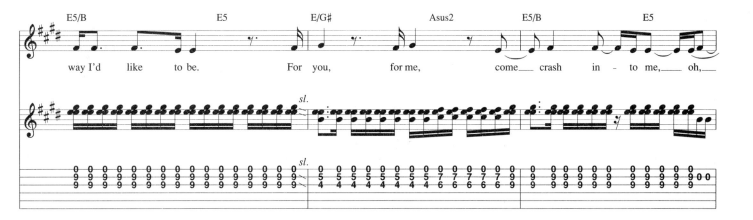

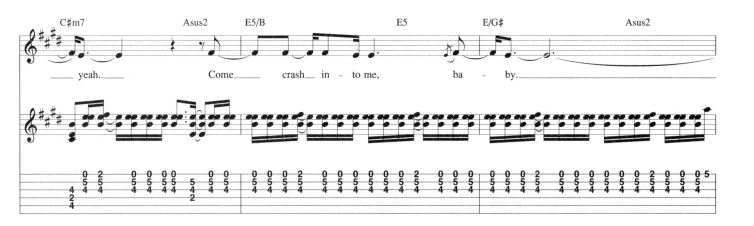

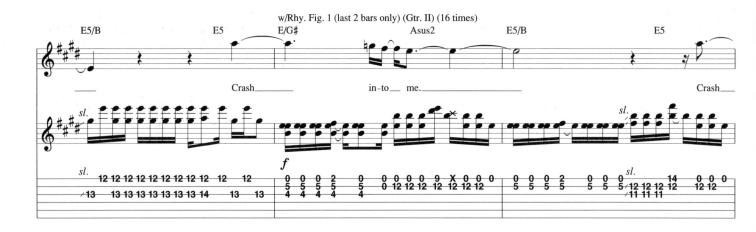

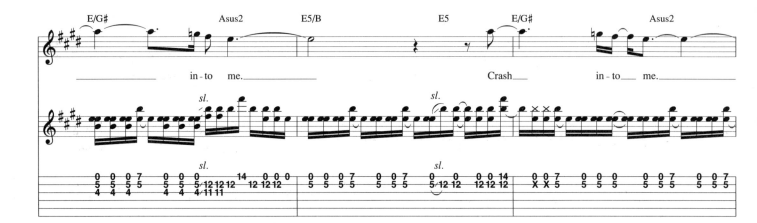

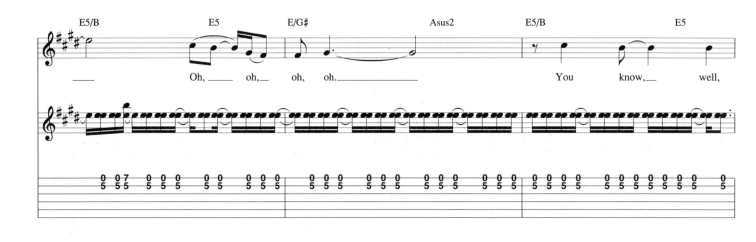

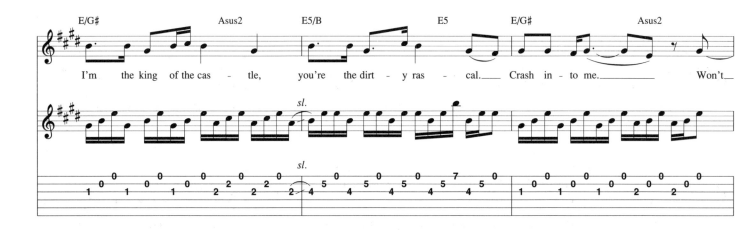

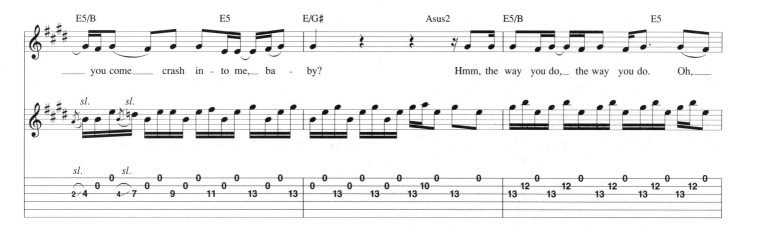

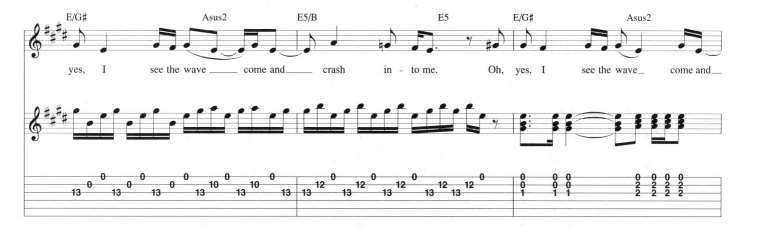

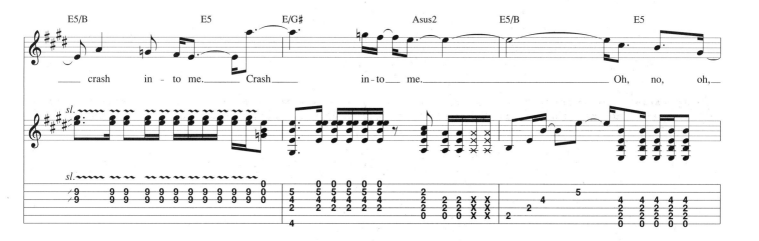

w/Rhy. Fig. 3 (12 times)

Additional Lyrics

3. Oh, if I've gone overboard,
   Then I'm begging you
   To forgive me, oh,
   In my haste.
   When I'm holding you up, girl,
   Close to me.
   And you come... *(To Chorus)*

DEED IS DONE

Words and Music by David J. Matthews, Carter Beauford,
Stefan Lessard, LeRoi Moore and Boyd Tinsley

1st, 2nd Verses
w/Rhy. Figs. 1 & 1A (both 12 times)
2nd time Gtr. II substitute Rhy. Fig. 1 (2 times)
N.C.
*

* 2nd time, sing w/variations ad lib.

w/Rhy. Fig. 1 (6 times) (Gtr. II)

2nd time Gtr. II substitute Riff A (7 1/2 times)

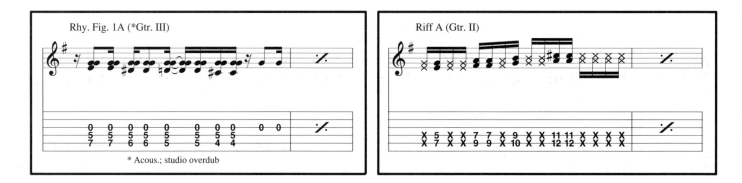

Rhy. Fig. 1A (*Gtr. III)

* Acous.; studio overdub

Riff A (Gtr. II)

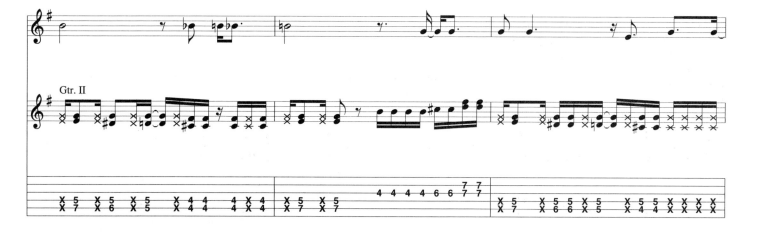

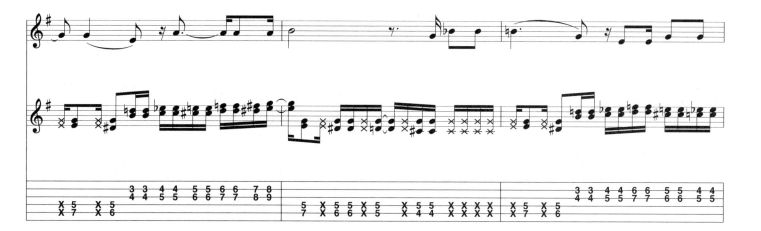

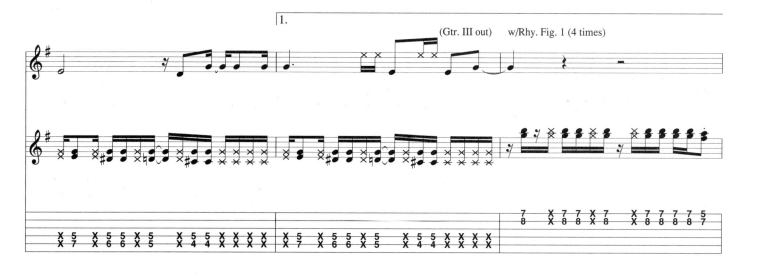

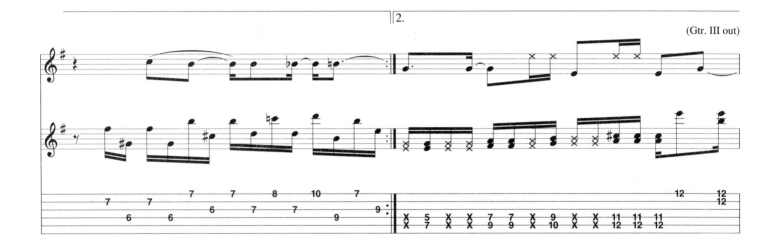

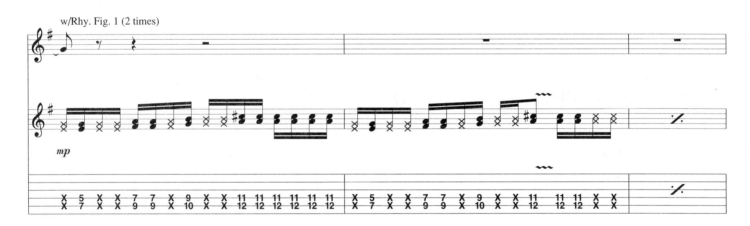

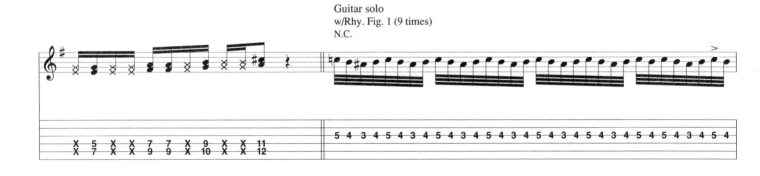

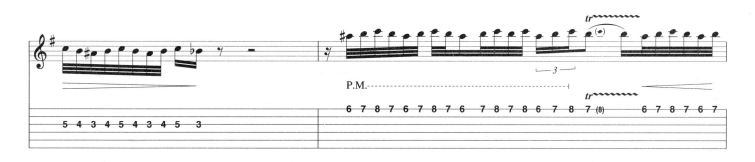

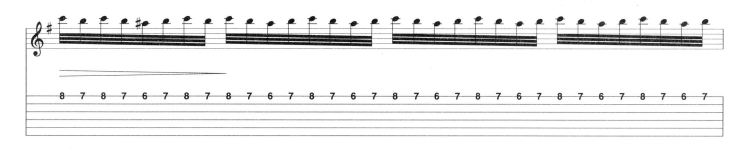

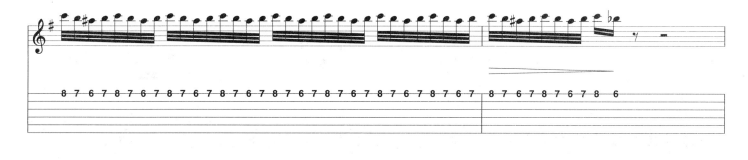

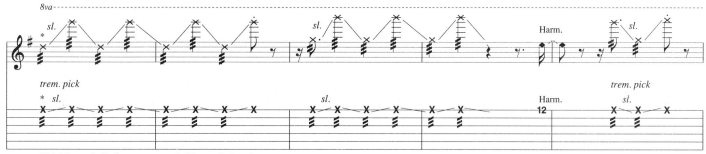

* Lightly rest L. H. finger on stg. and slide past fretboard.

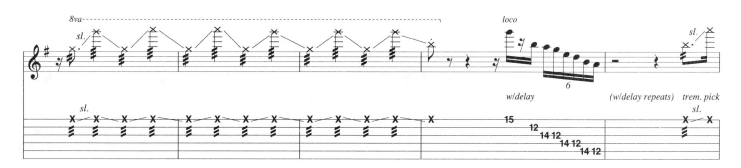

WHAT WOULD YOU SAY

Words and Music by
David J. Matthews

*Play all guitar figures w/slight variations ad lib when
recalled (throughout).

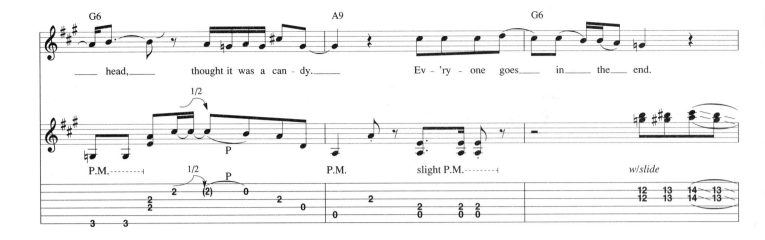

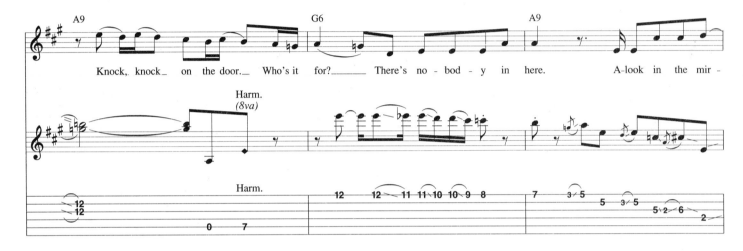

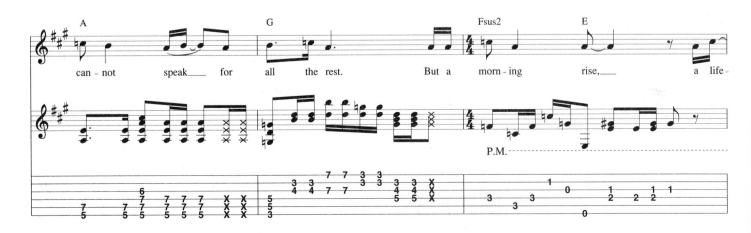

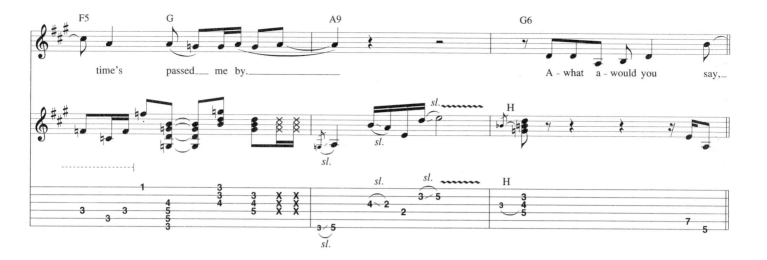

time's passed me by. A - what a - would you say,

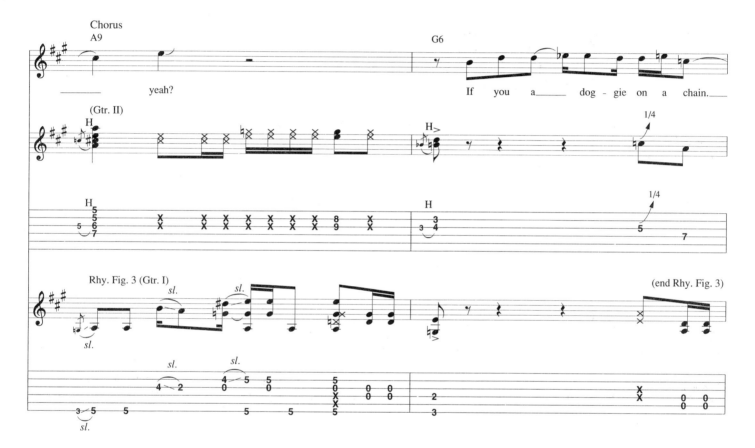

Chorus

yeah? If you a dog - gie on a chain.

(Gtr. II)

Rhy. Fig. 3 (Gtr. I) (end Rhy. Fig. 3)

w/Rhy. Fig. 3 (6½ times)

If you a mon - key on a string.

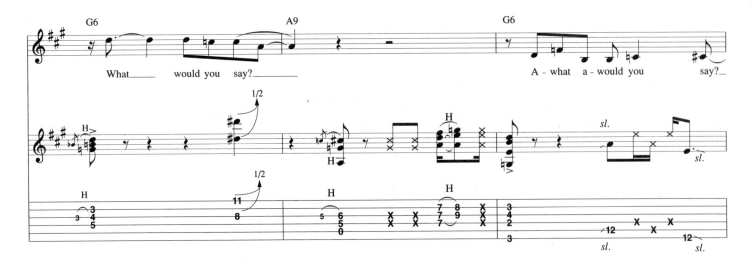

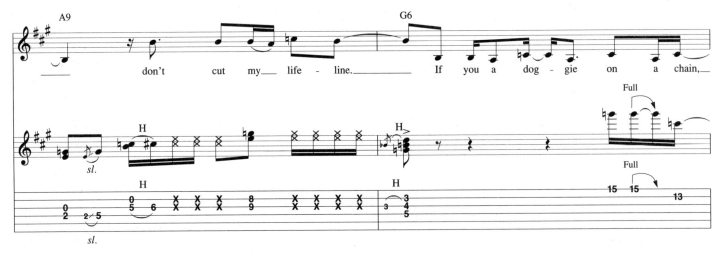

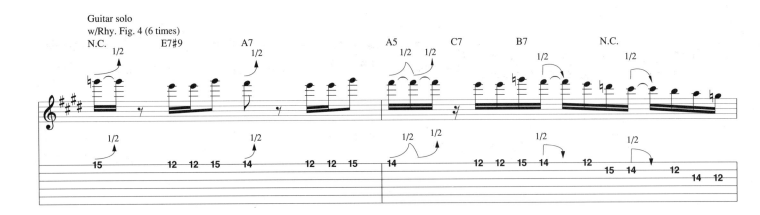

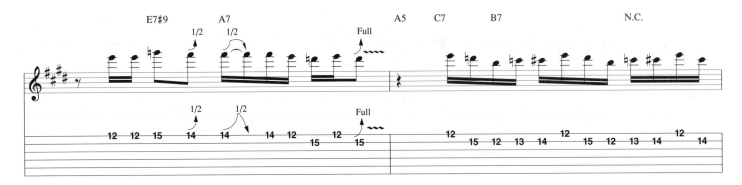

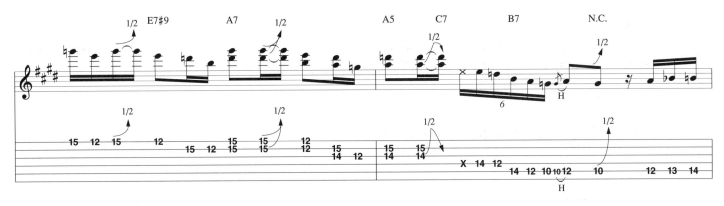

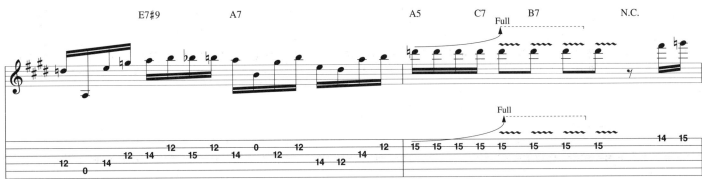

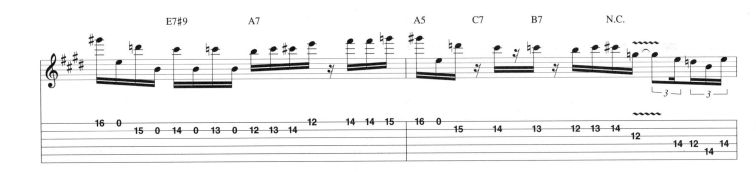

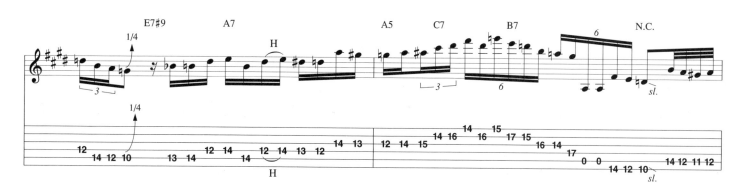

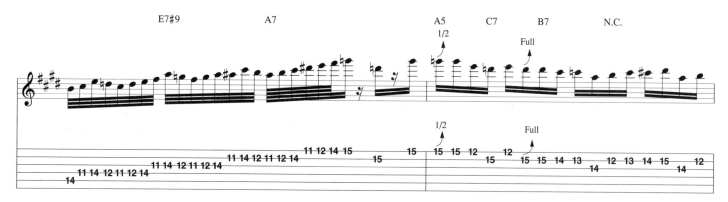

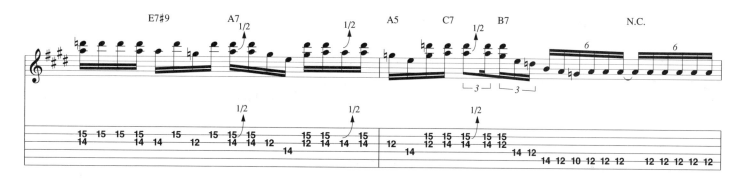

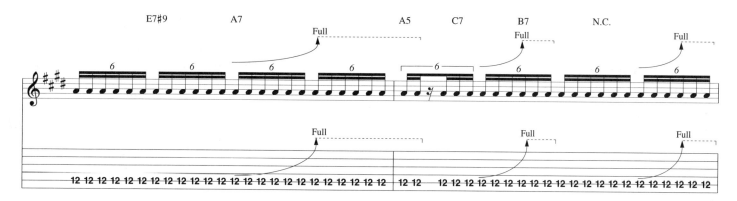

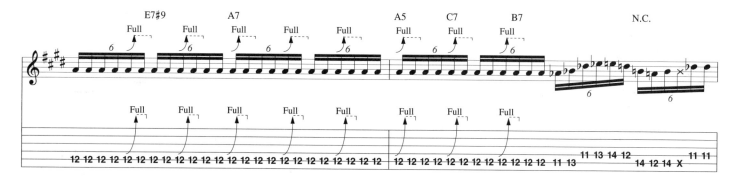

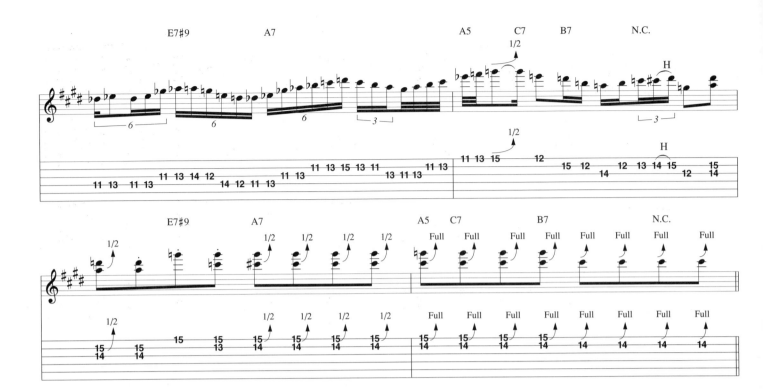

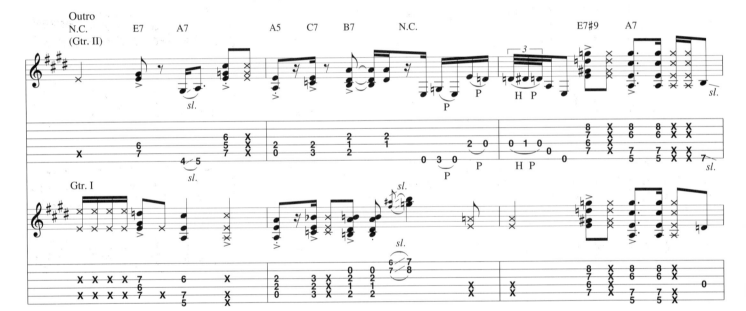

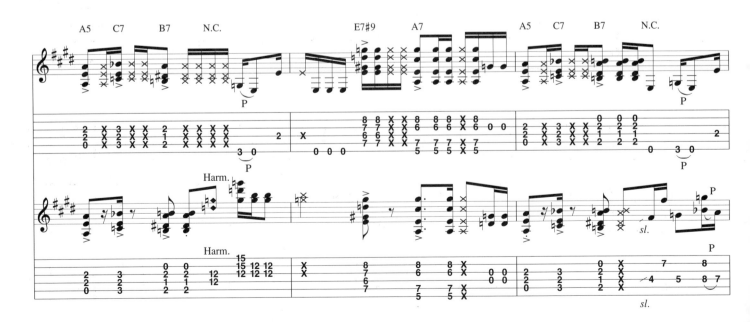

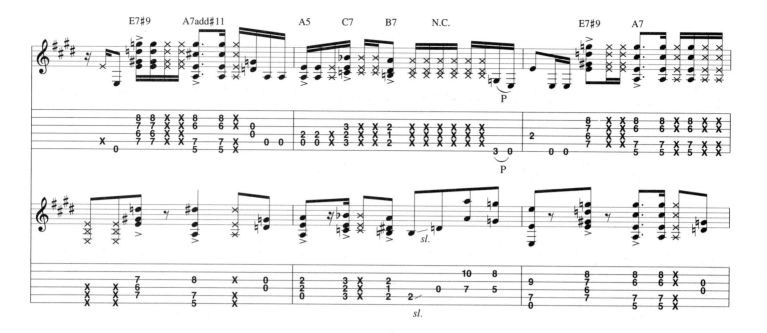

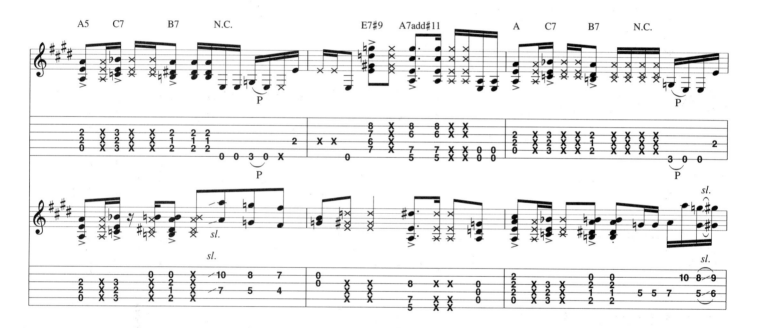

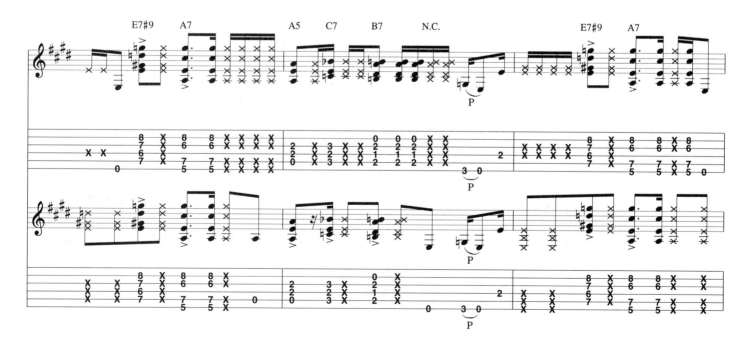

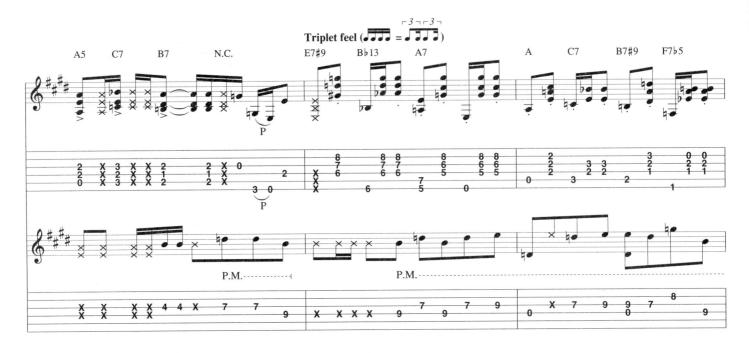

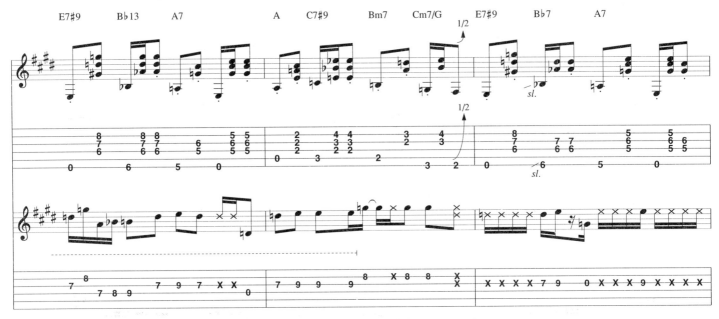

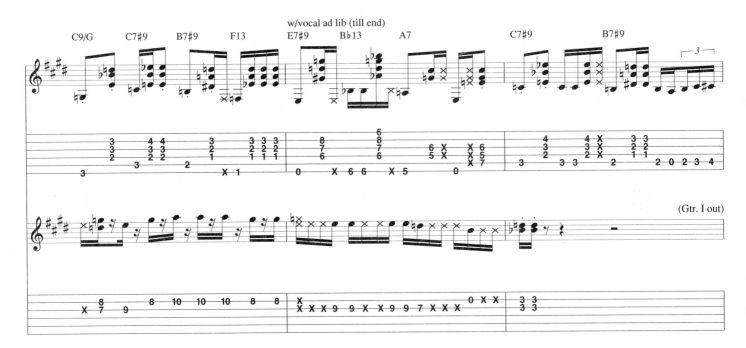

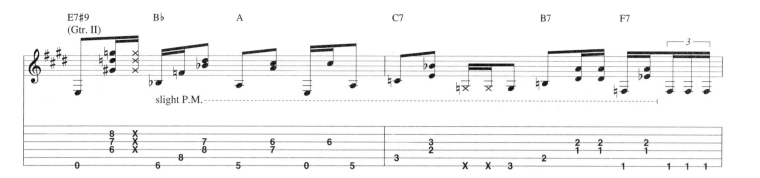

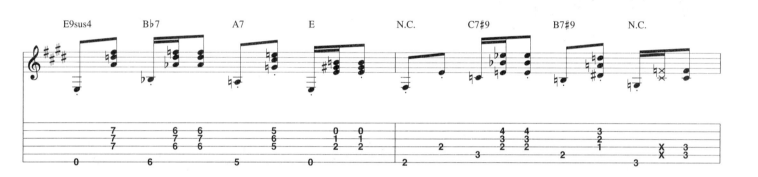

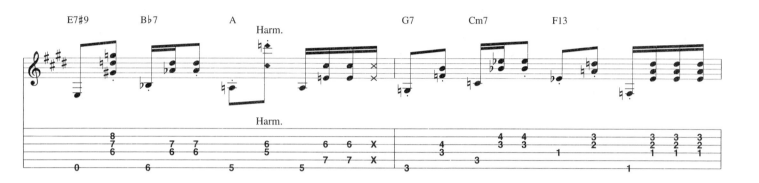

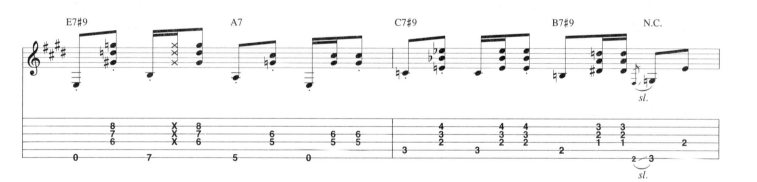

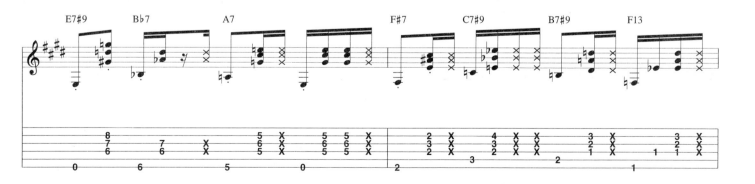

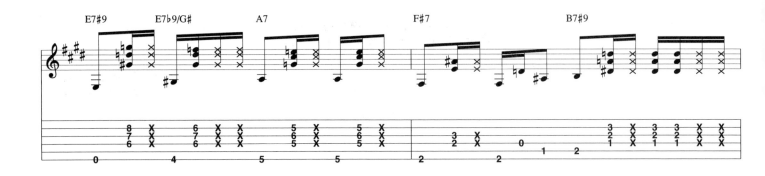

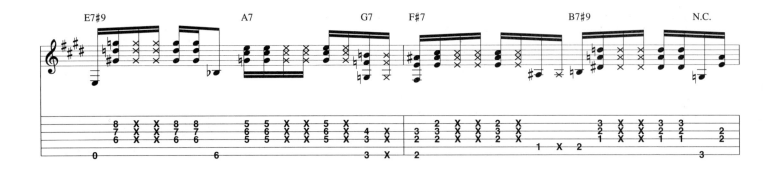

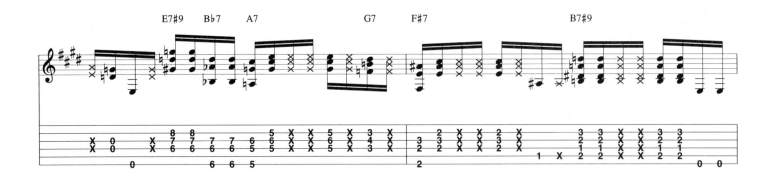

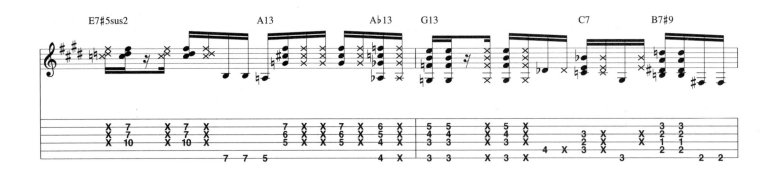

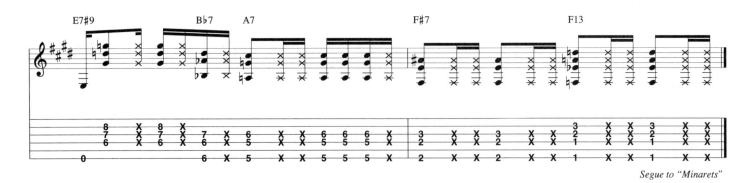

Segue to "Minarets"

MINARETS

Words and Music by
David J. Matthews

*
w/slide
w/delay

steady gliss.

* Indicates vol. pedal (throughout).

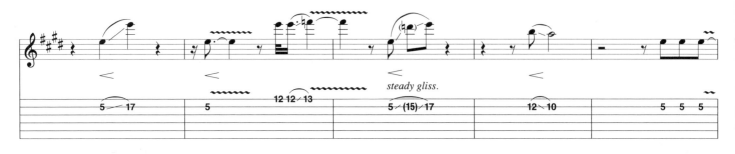

steady gliss.

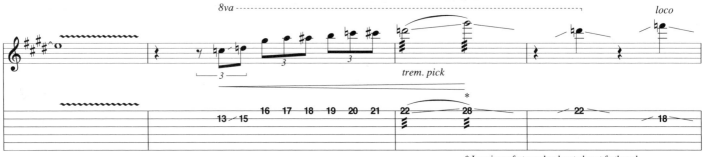

8va -

loco

trem. pick

*

* Imaginary fret number located past fretboard.

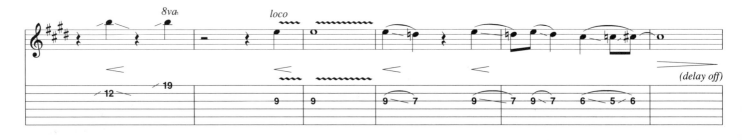

8va

loco

(delay off)

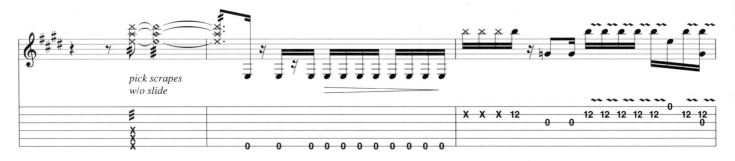

pick scrapes
w/o slide

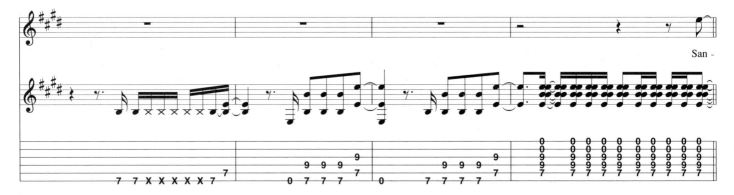

San -

60

1st Verse
w/Rhy. Fig. 1 (3 times)

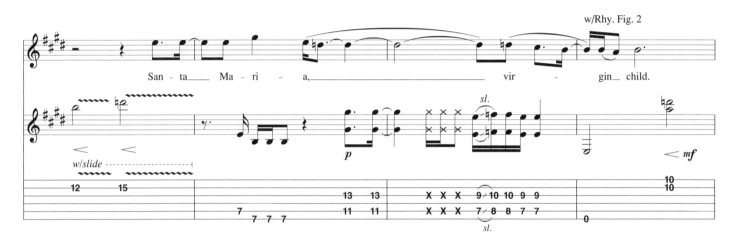

ta Ma - ri - a,_____ choose_____ your chil - dren.

w/Rhy. Fig. 2

San - ta____ Ma - ri - a,_____ vir - gin__ child.

Chorus

F/E   E   Amaj9   (end Rhy. Fig. 3A)

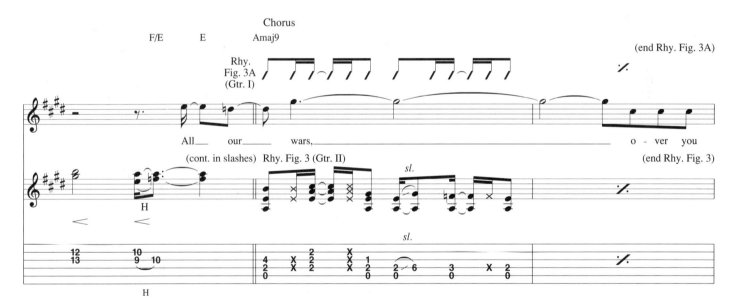

All____ our____ wars,_____ o - ver you

(cont. in slashes) Rhy. Fig. 3 (Gtr. II)   (end Rhy. Fig. 3)

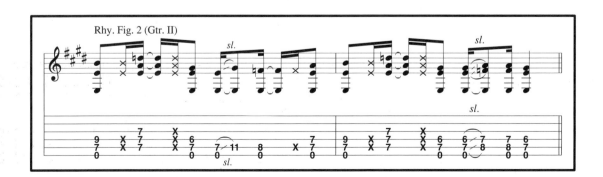

2nd Verse
w/Rhy. Fig. 1 (3 times)

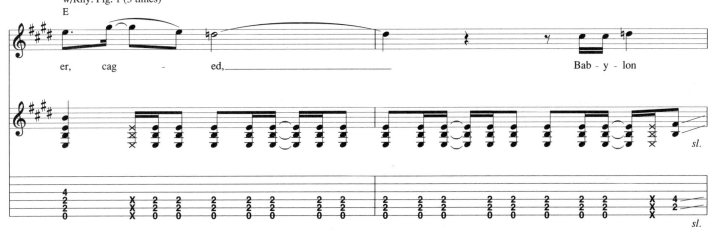

er,   cag - ed,_____   Bab - y - lon

will   fall.   Sis -

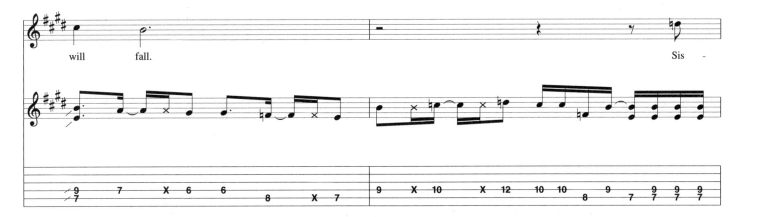

ter,   chained_ and   bound,_____   beat - en

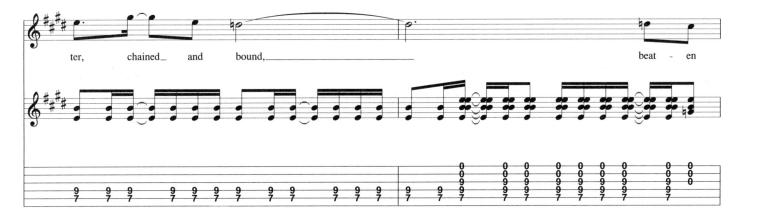

w/Rhy. Fig. 2

and   bleed - ing_____   heart._____   The T -

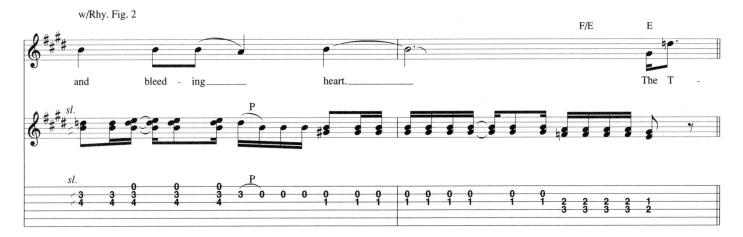

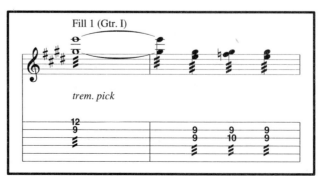

Interlude
w/Rhy. Fig. 1

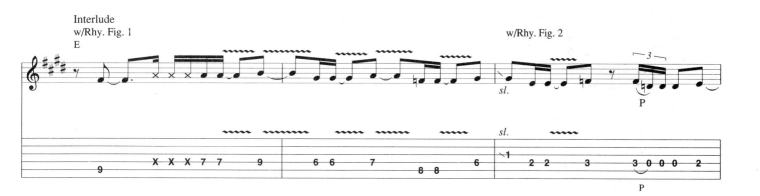

w/Rhy. Fig. 3

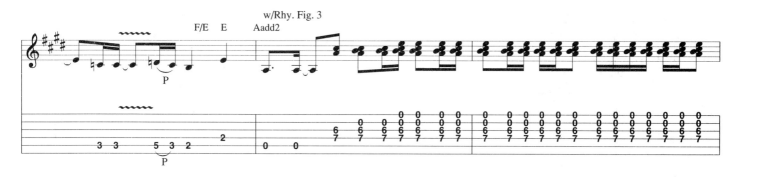

w/Rhy. Fig. 2
w/voc. ad lib (next 4 bars)

w/Rhy. Fig. 3
Aadd2

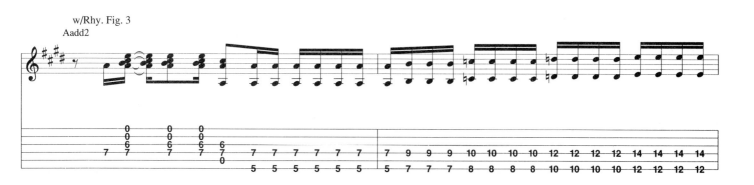

w/Rhy. Fig. 2
E

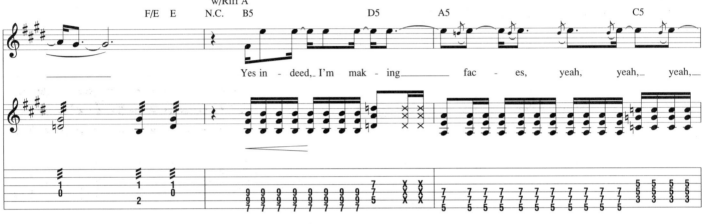

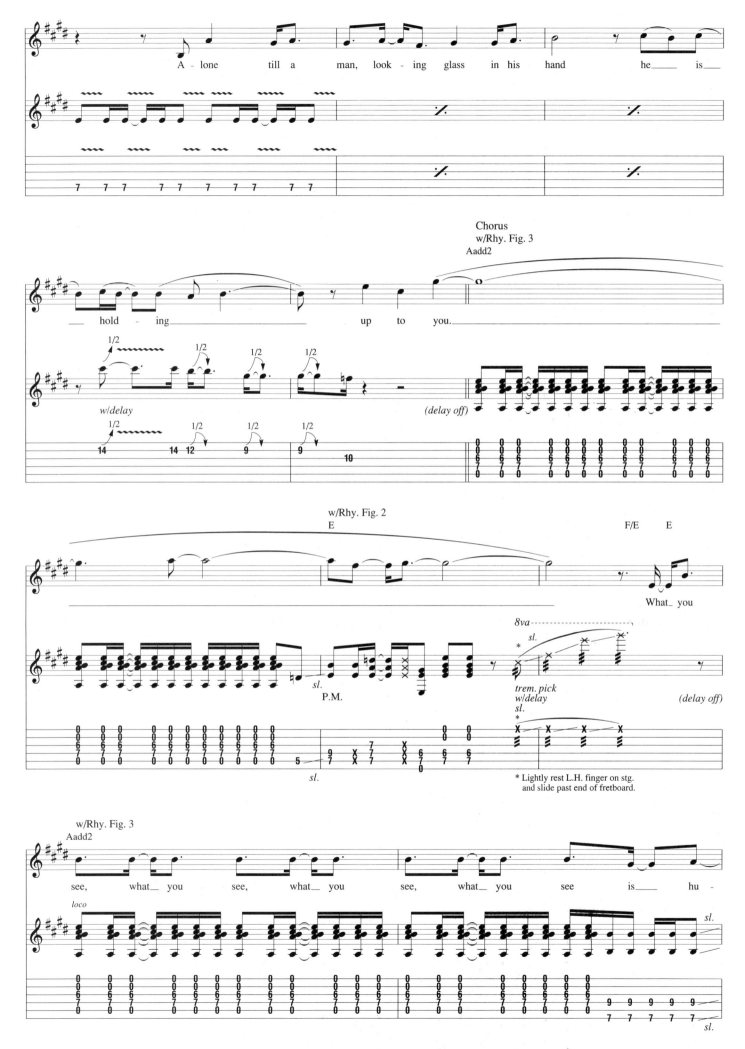

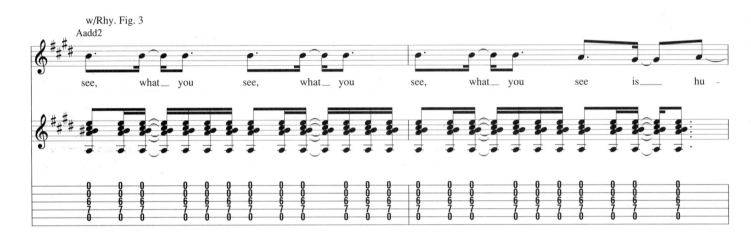

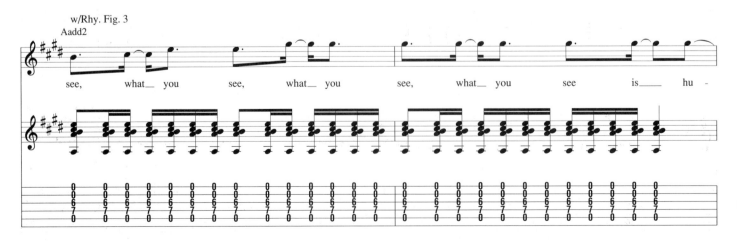

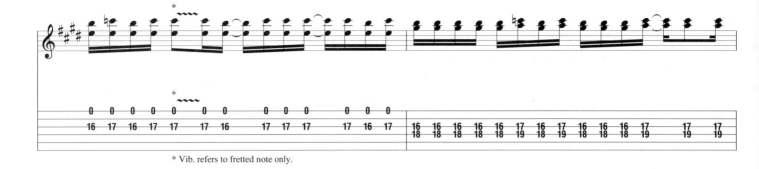

* Vib. refers to fretted note only.

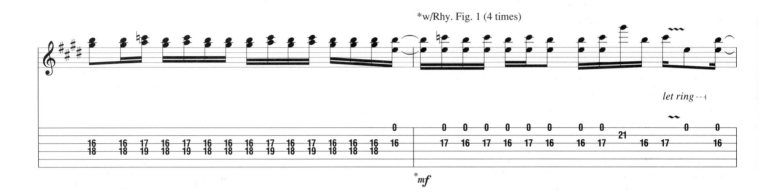

*w/Rhy. Fig. 1 (4 times)

let ring

*mf

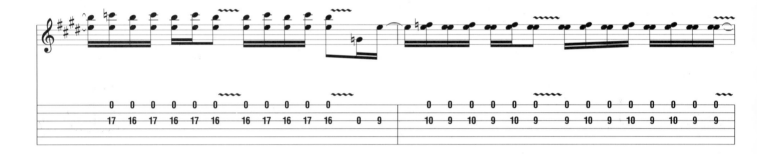

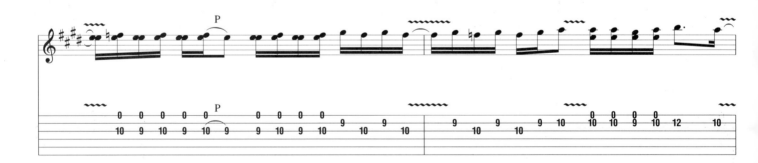

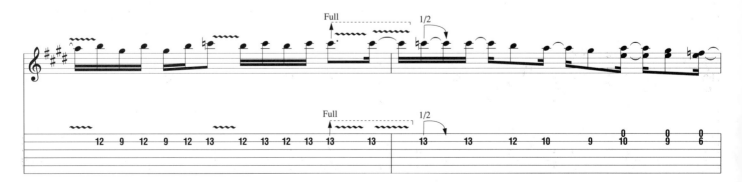

* Artificial harmonics achieved by lightly touching stg. w/R.H. index finger at fret indicated
in parentheses and picking from behind. (Pick held between thumb and middle finger.)

STREAM

**Words and Music by
Tim Reynolds**

Drop D tuning:
⑥= D

Freely ♩ = ca 88

* 𝄋 ****Moderately fast** ♩ = 140

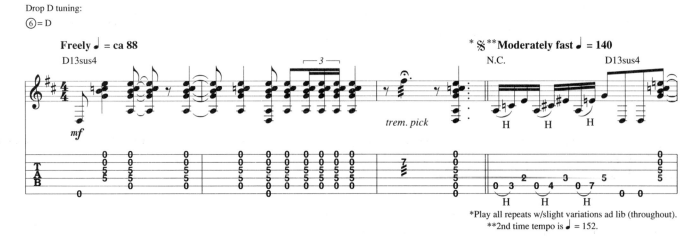

*Play all repeats w/slight variations ad lib (throughout).
**2nd time tempo is ♩ = 152.

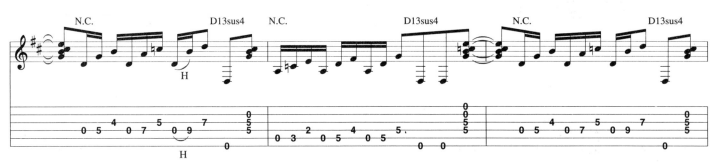

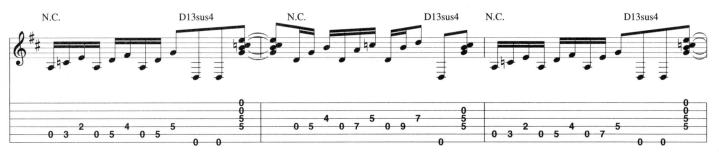

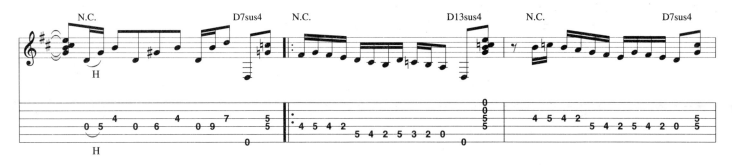

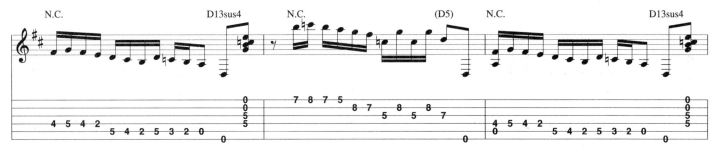

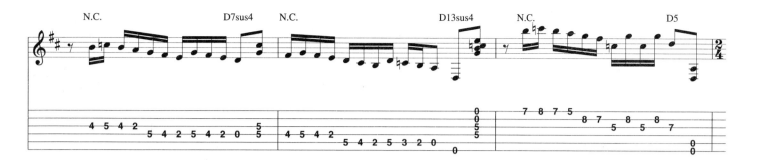

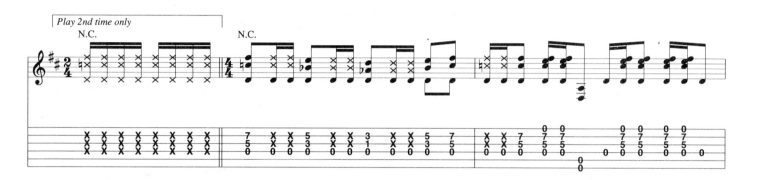

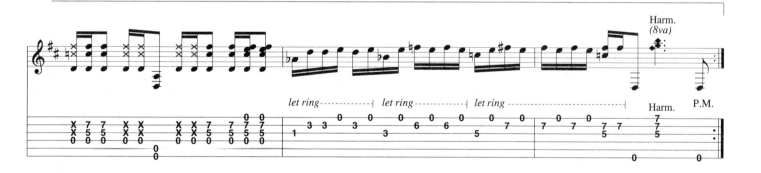

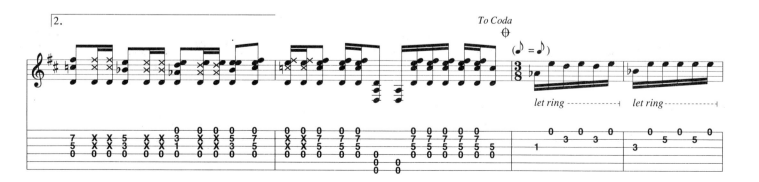

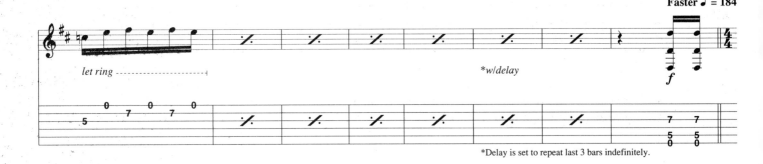

Faster ♩ = 184

*w/delay

*Delay is set to repeat last 3 bars indefinitely.

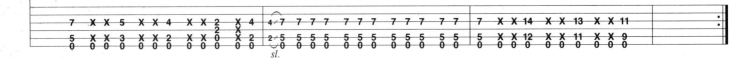

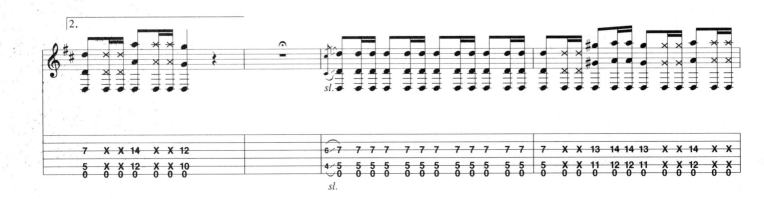

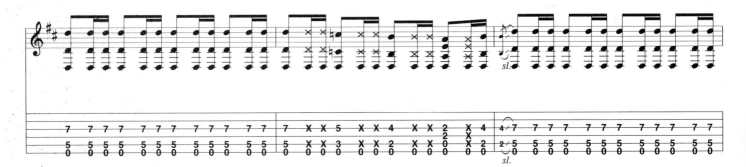

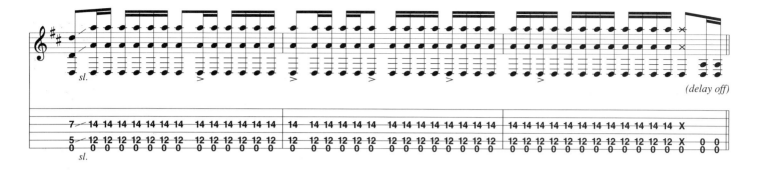

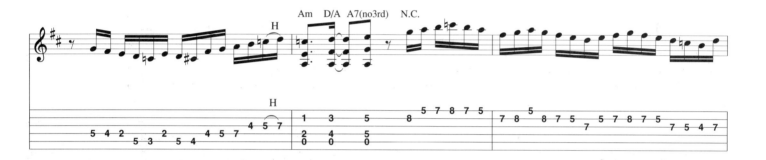

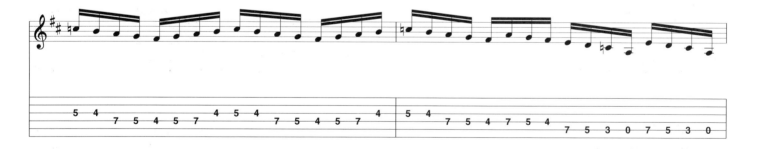

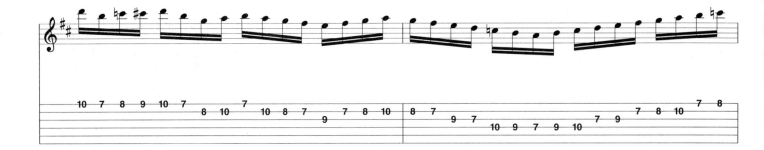

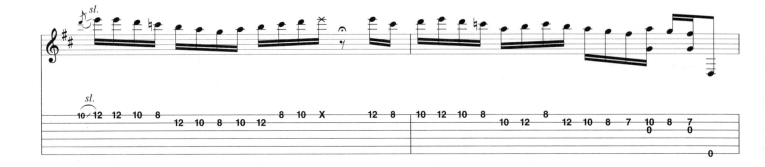

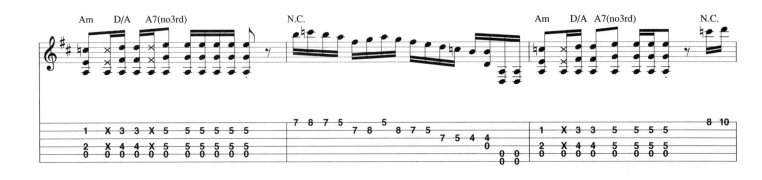

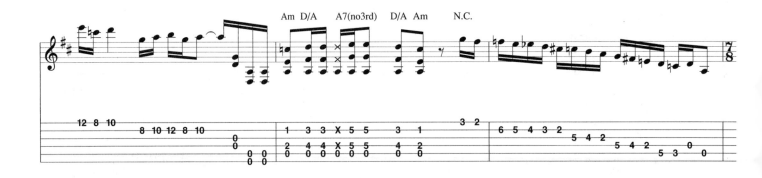

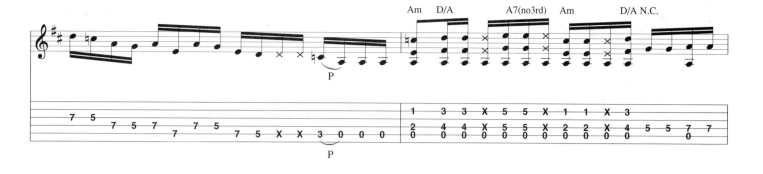

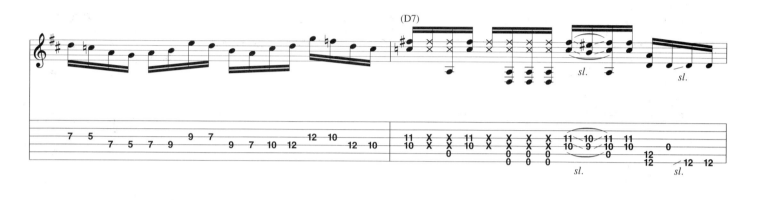

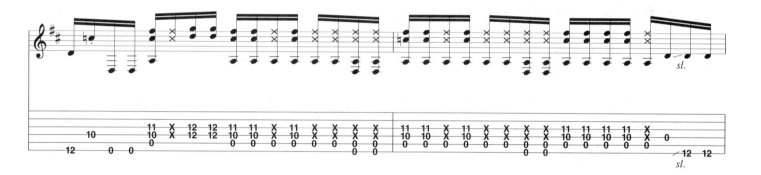

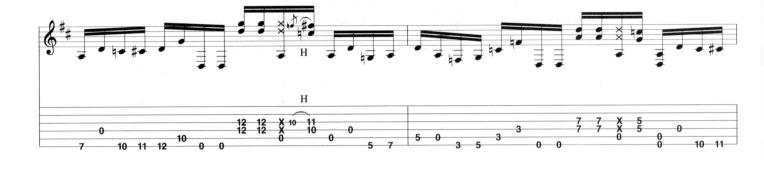

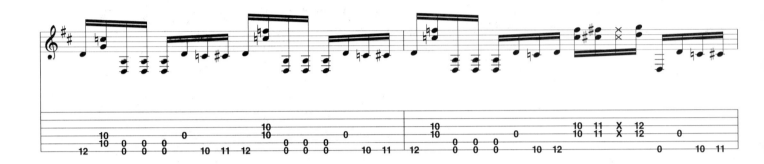

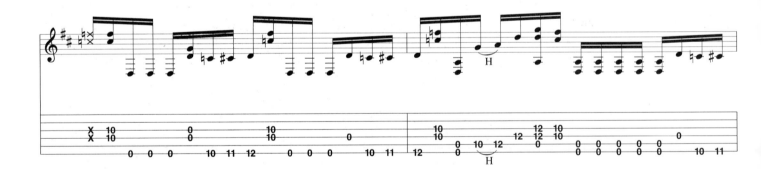

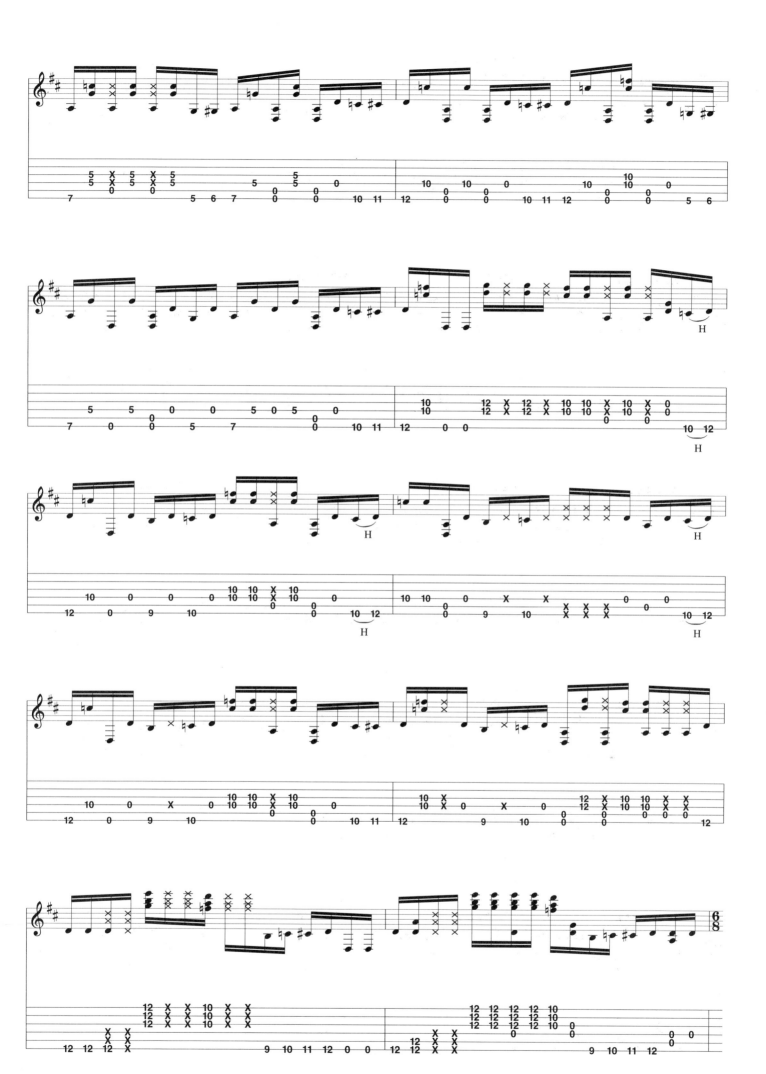

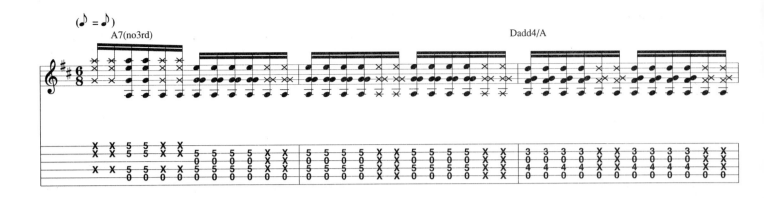

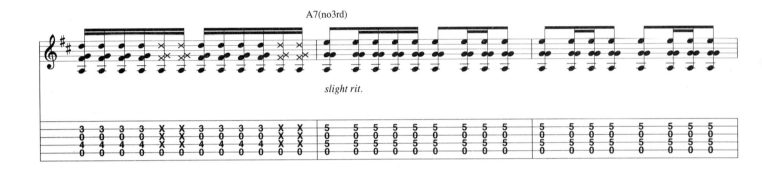

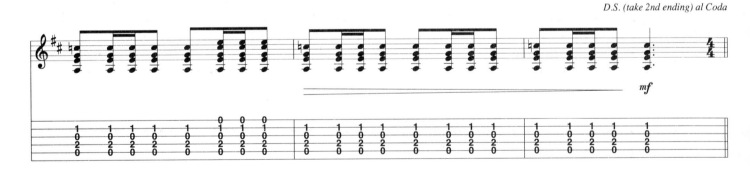

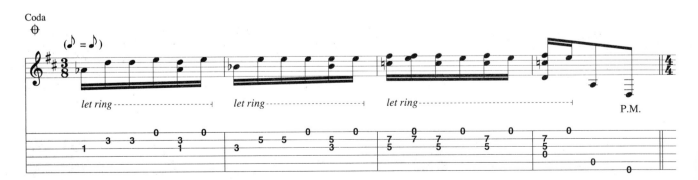

Slightly faster ♩ = 160

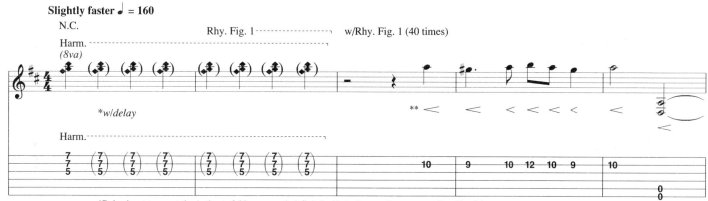

*Delay is set to repeat the 1st beat of this measure indefinitely. Notes in parentheses are produced by delay.
**Vol. pedal swells.

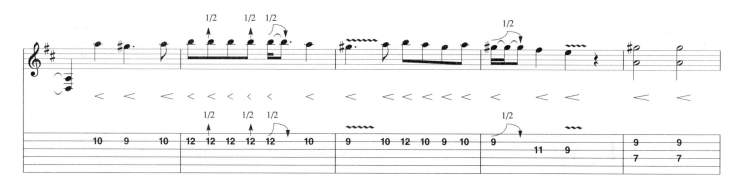

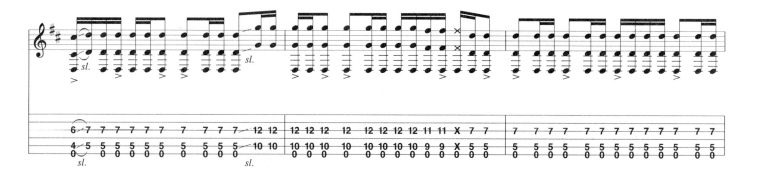

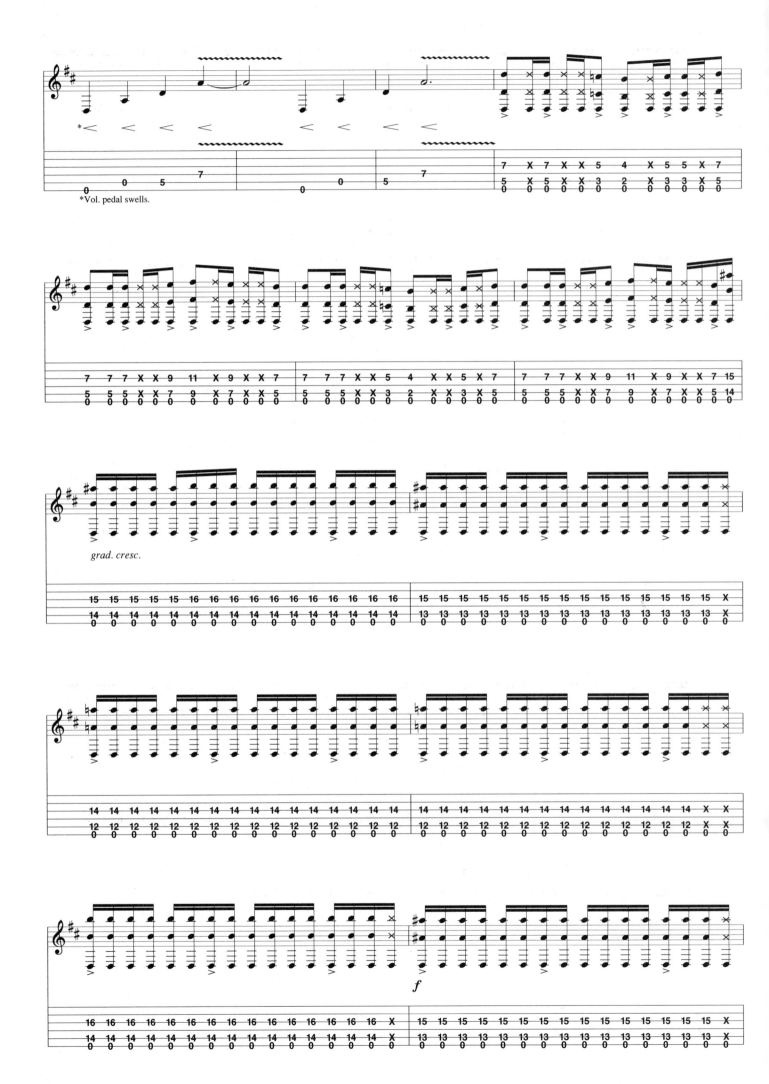

*Vol. pedal swells.

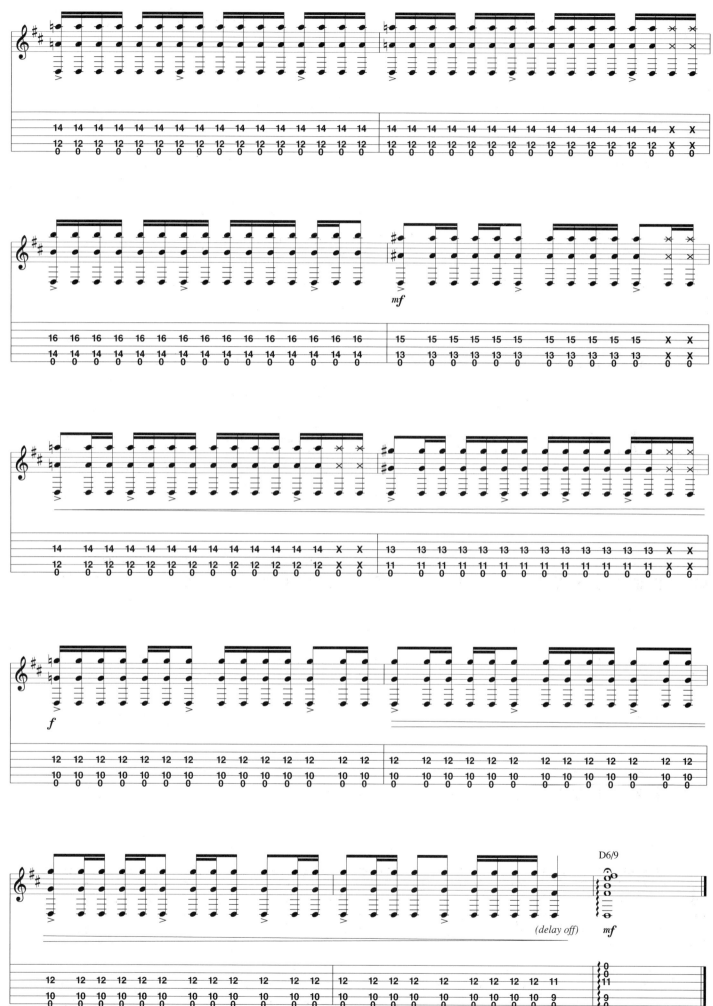

CHRISTMAS SONG

Words and Music by
David J. Matthews

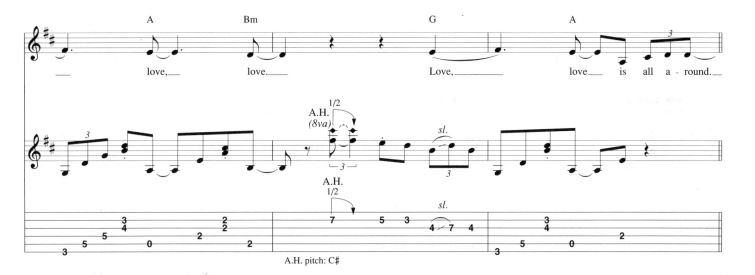

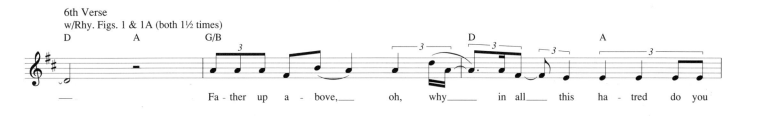

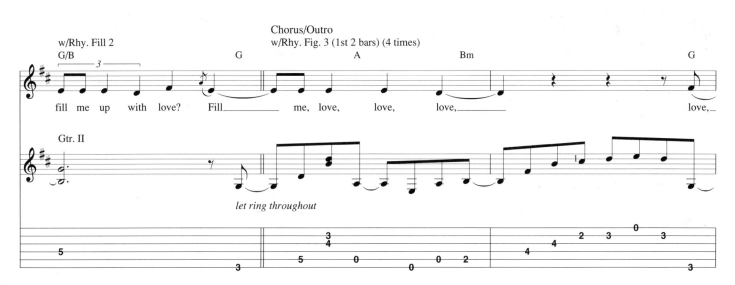

* Bend executed by pushing
down on stg. behind nut.

SEEK UP

Words and Music by
David J. Matthews

* Play all gtr. parts w/slight variations ad lib when repeated or recalled (throughout).
** Acous.

* Drop-D tuning: ⑥ = D

* Refers to notes played by L.H. only.

w/Rhy. Fig. 2 — B♭   C   w/Rhy. Fig. 1 — Dm   w/Rhy. Fig. 2 — B♭

Fall_____ back_____ a - gain.   Fall_____

let ring

* Indicates vol. pedal (throughout).

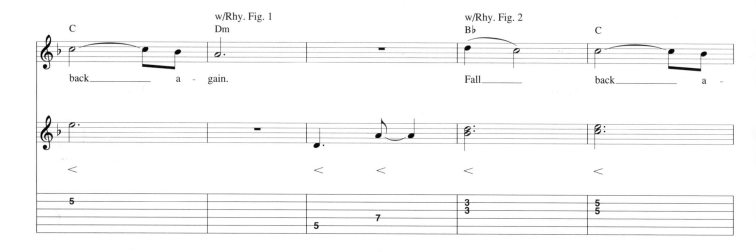

C   w/Rhy. Fig. 1 — Dm   w/Rhy. Fig. 2 — B♭   C

back_____ a - gain.   Fall_____ back_____ a -

w/Rhy. Fig. 1 — Dm   w/Rhy. Fig. 2 — B♭   C

gain.   Fall_____ back_____ a -

* let ring-----------------

* Refers to notes played by L.H. only.

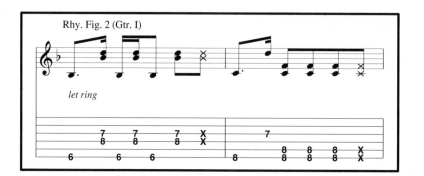

Rhy. Fig. 2 (Gtr. I)

let ring

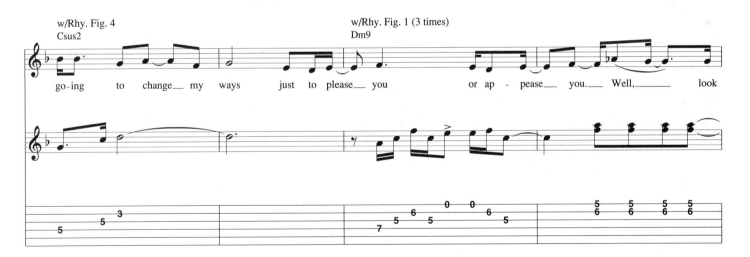

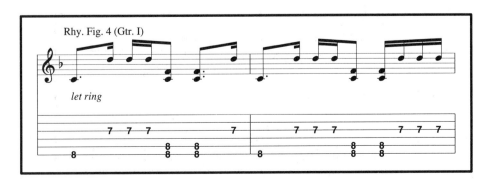

at this crowd,___ five___ bil - lion___ proud,___ will - ing to punch it out.___ Right, wrong,___

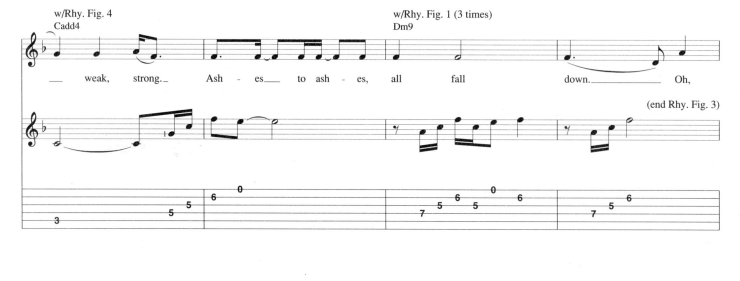

w/Rhy. Fig. 4
Cadd4

w/Rhy. Fig. 1 (3 times)
Dm9

___ weak, strong.___ Ash - es___ to ash - es, all fall down._____ Oh,

(end Rhy. Fig. 3)

look a - round___ a - bout___ this round, a - bout___ this mer - ry - go - round___ and a - round. If at all___

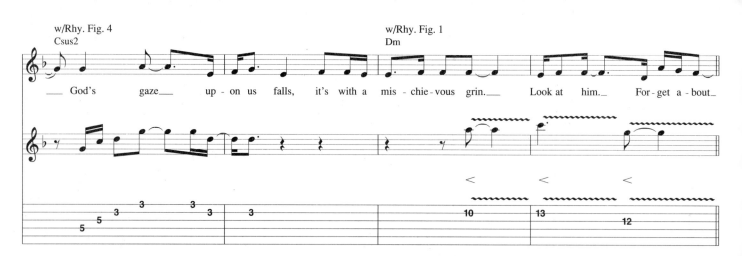

w/Rhy. Fig. 4
Csus2

w/Rhy. Fig. 1
Dm

___ God's gaze___ up - on us falls, it's with a mis - chie - vous grin. Look at him.___ For - get a - bout___

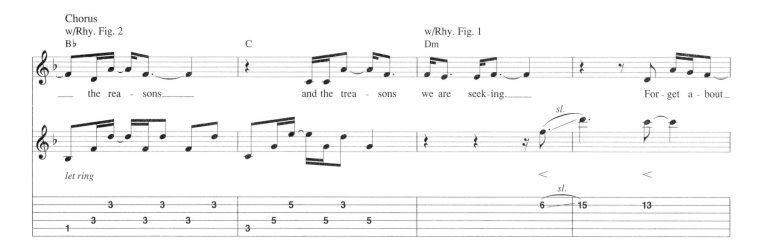

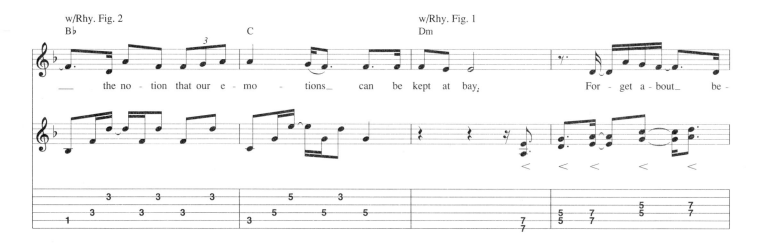

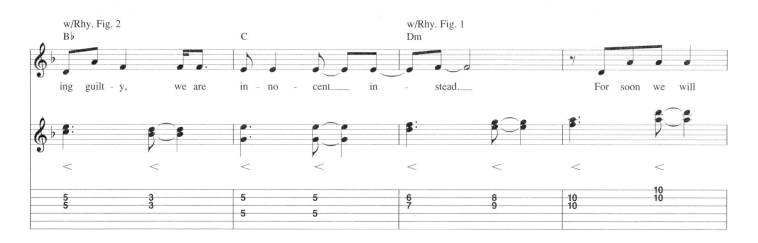

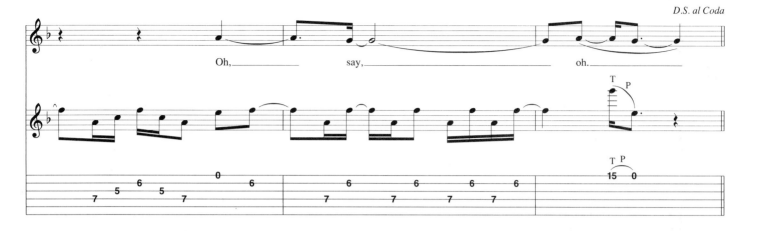

Oh,_____ say,_____ oh.

Coda (w/last bar of Rhy. Fig. 5)

Bridge
w/Rhy. Fig. 6 (6 times)

Oh.____ You seek up an e - mo - tion - and__ your cup is o - ver -

Gtr. II

w/voc. ad lib (next 4 bars)

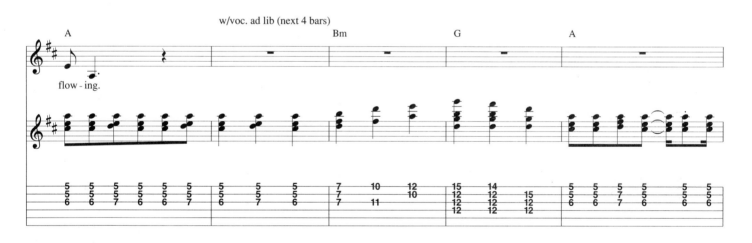

flow - ing.

w/voc. ad lib (next 4 bars)

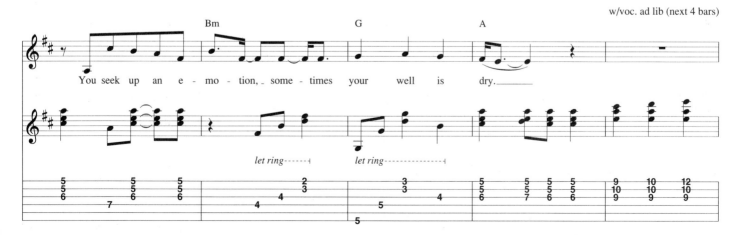

You seek up an e - mo - tion, some - times your well is dry.____

let ring------   let ring---------------

101

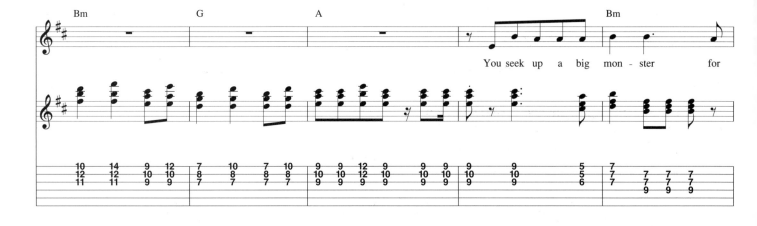

You seek up a big mon-ster for

w/voc. ad lib (next 4 bars)

him to fight__ your wars__ for you.__

let ring

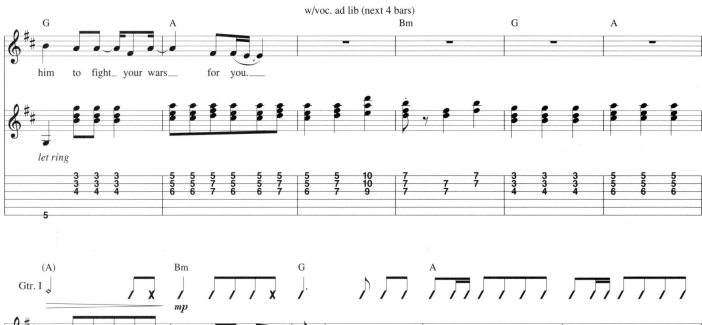

Gtr. I

But when he find his way to you,__ the dev-il's not go-ing. Ha, ha,__ ha, ha.__

w/Rhy. Fill 1 (Gtr. I)
B5   N.C.

w/Rhy. Fig. 1 (2 times)
Dm9

**

Ah._____

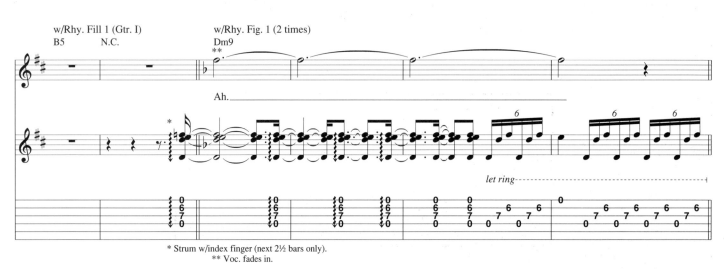

let ring

* Strum w/index finger (next 2½ bars only).
** Voc. fades in.

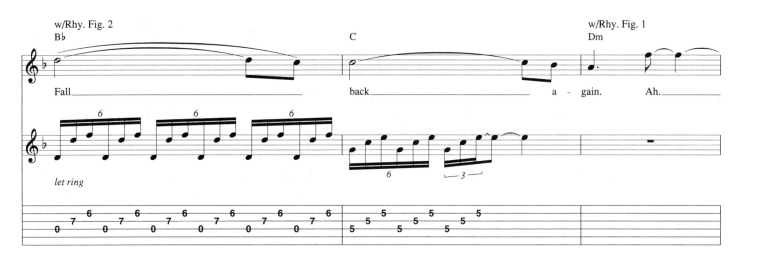

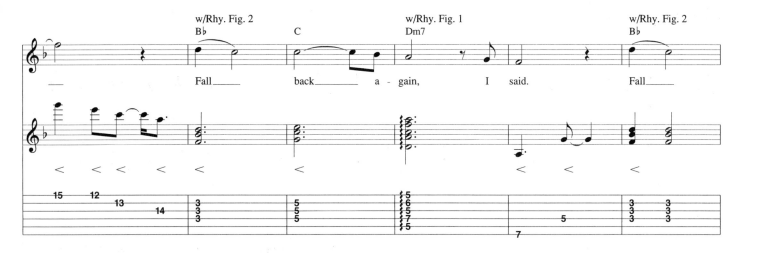

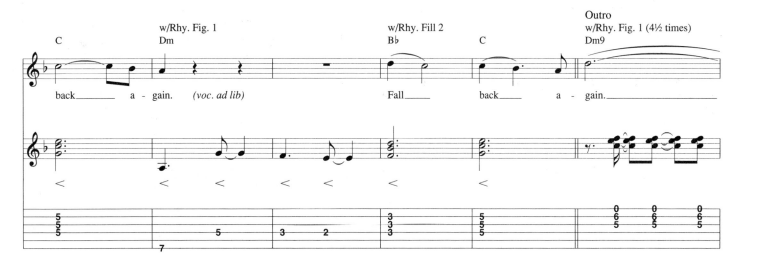

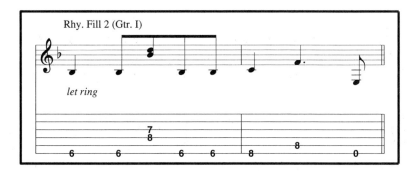

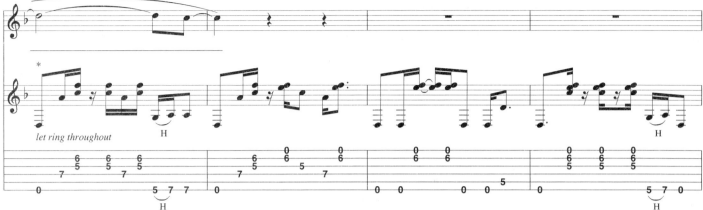

let ring throughout

* Slap 6th stg. w/R.H. thumb (next 20 bars).

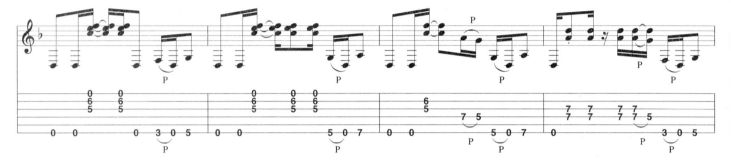

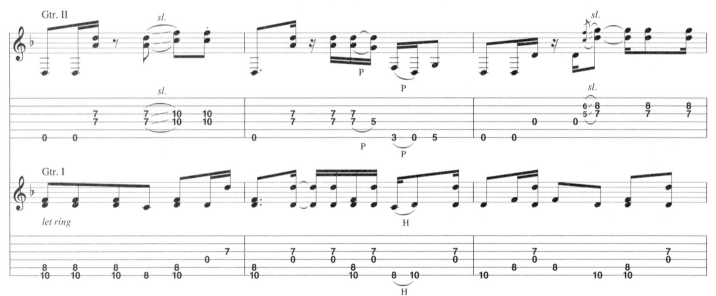

Gtr. II

Gtr. I

let ring

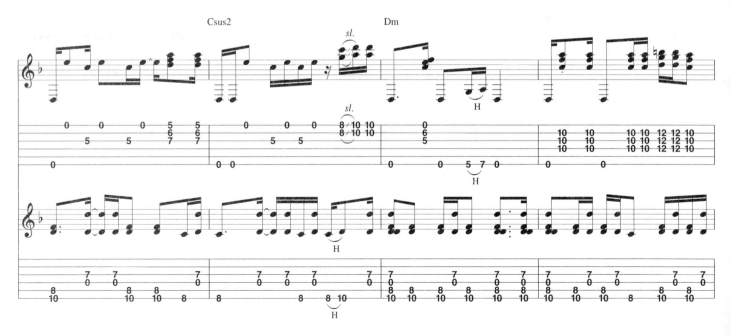

Csus2

Dm

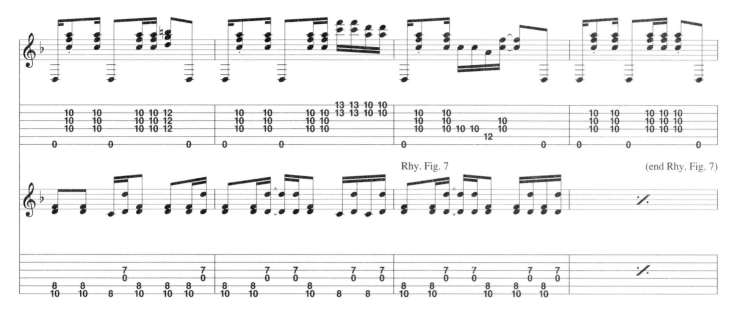

Rhy. Fig. 7   (end Rhy. Fig. 7)

w/Rhy. Fig. 7 (4 times)
Gtr. II

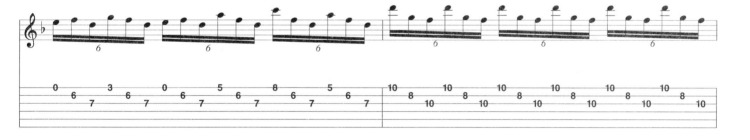

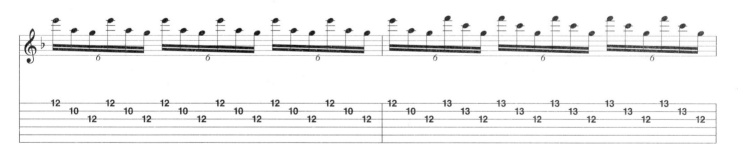

* w/Rhy. Fig. 1 (2 times)

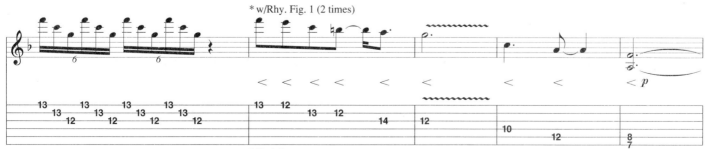

* Grad. decresc.

105

Additional Lyrics

3. Late at night with TV's hungry child,
   His belly swelled.
   Well, for the price of a Coke or a smoke,
   I could keep alive those hungry eyes.
   Man, take a look again, take a look again,
   Take a look again.
   Every day things change,
   Basically they stay the same. *(To Chorus)*

ANTS MARCHING

Words and Music by
David J. Matthews

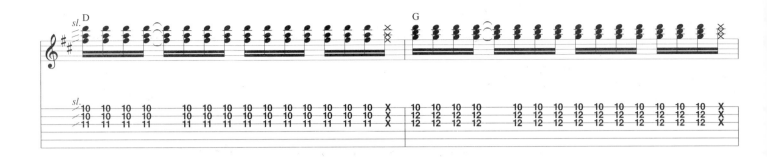

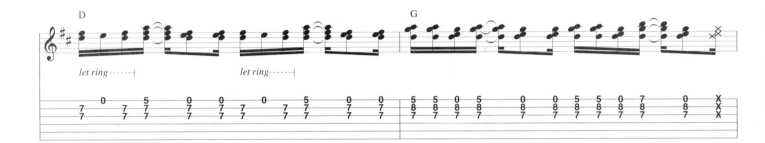

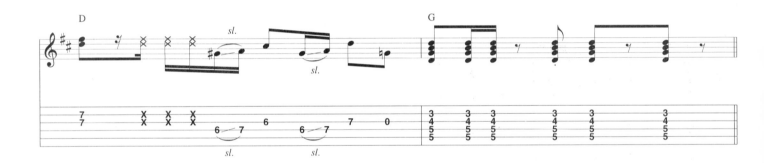

3rd Verse
w/Rhy. Fig. 1 (2 times) (Gtrs. I & II)

Driv - ing a - long this high - way, all these cars and up - on the side - walk,

w/last bar of Rhy. Fig. 1 (Gtr. I)

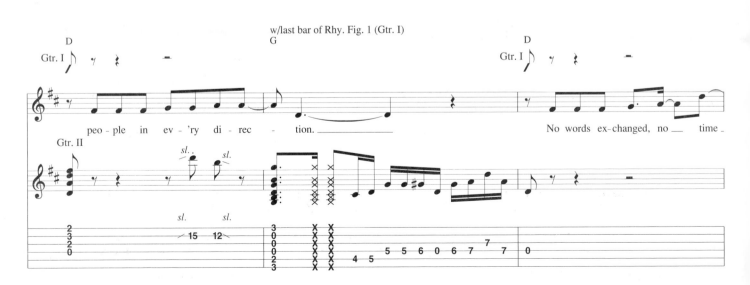

peo - ple in ev - 'ry di - rec - tion. No words ex - changed, no time

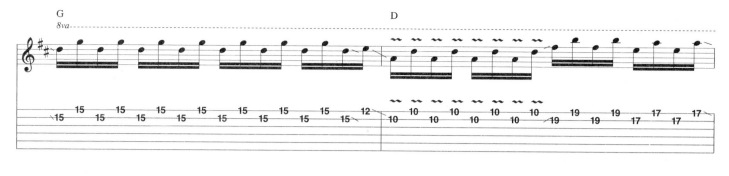

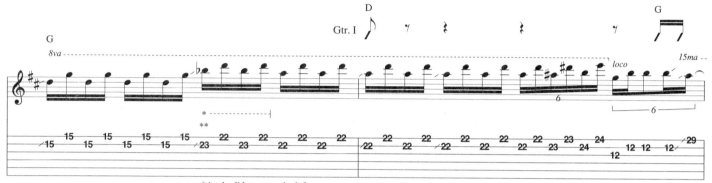

*Angle slide to cover both frets.
**All fret numbers above 22 are imaginary and are located past fretboard.

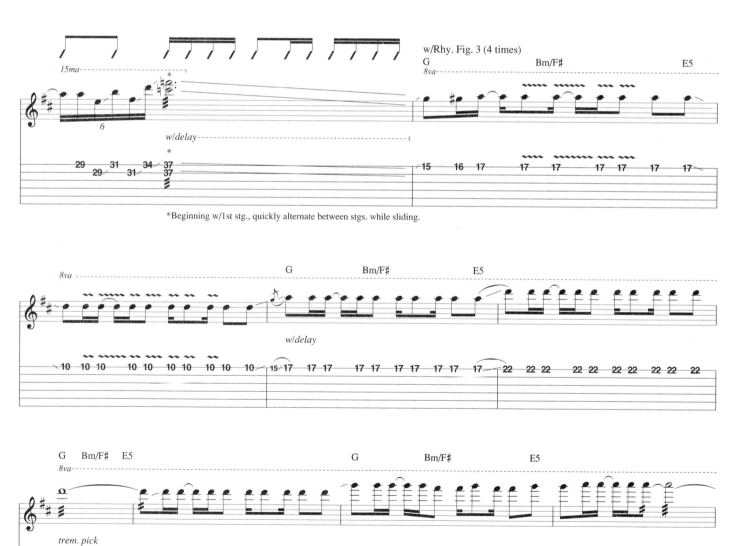

*Beginning w/1st stg., quickly alternate between stgs. while sliding.

*Pick in 16th note rhythm
while sliding (next 2 bars).

w/Rhy. Fig. 1 (4 times)

Lights___ down,___ you up and die.___

LITTLE THING

Words and Music by
David J. Matthews

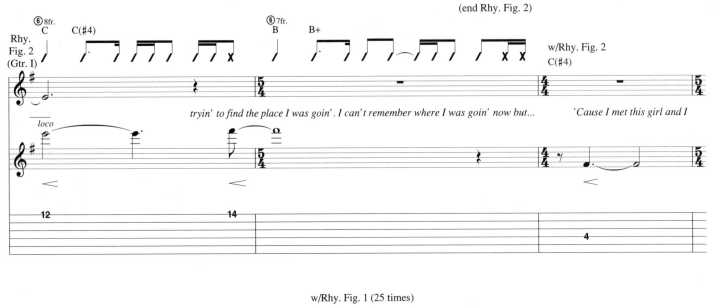

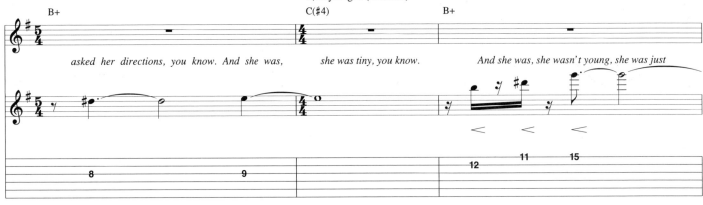

*Lightly touch stg. w/L.H. finger approx. where
24th fret would be and slide up and down as
indicated.

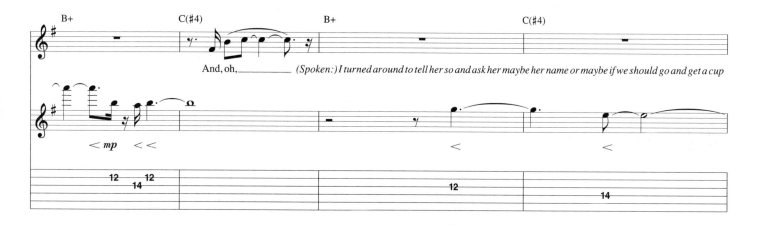

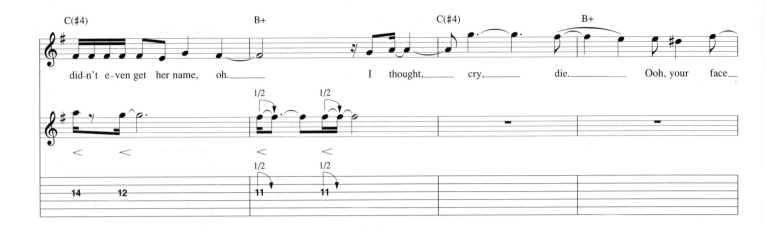

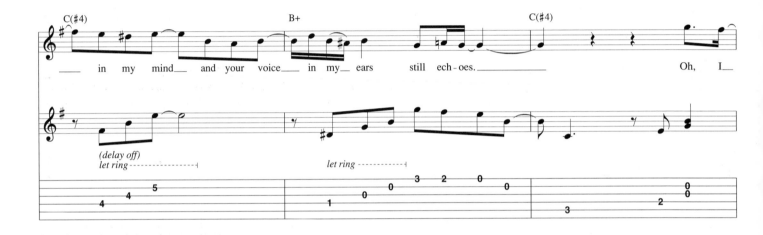

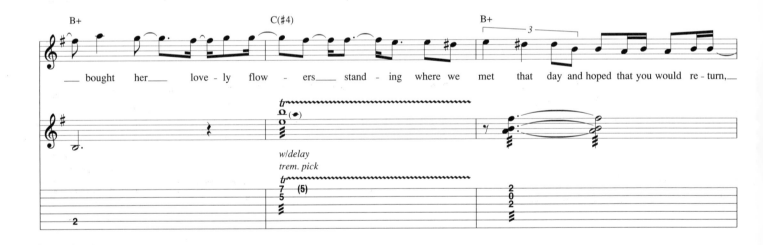

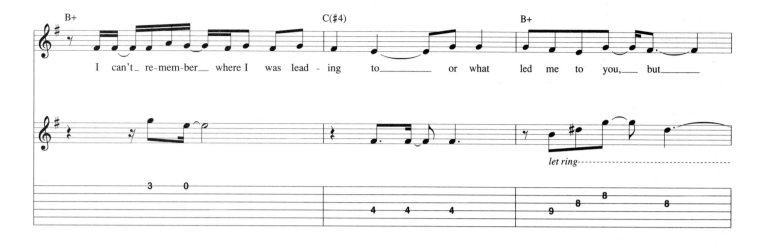

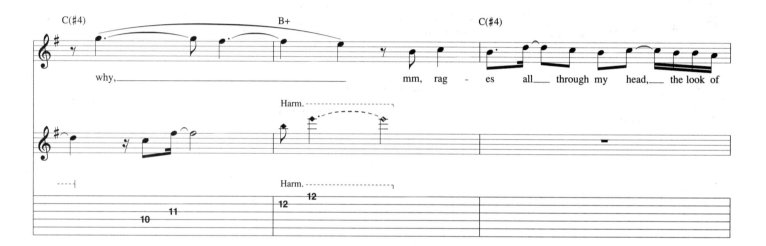

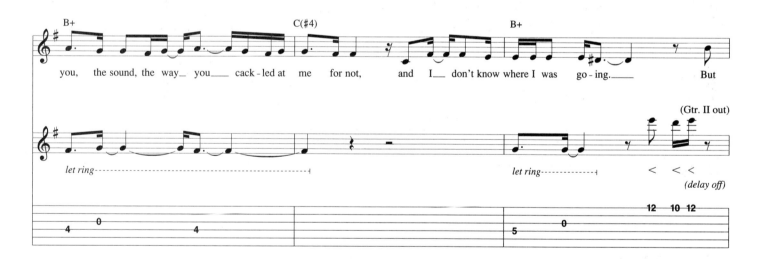

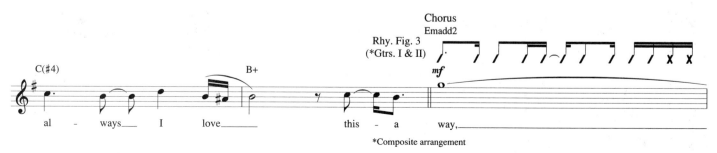

*Pick near bridge till end of bar.

Chorus
w/Rhy. Fig. 3 (3¾ times) (Gtr. I)
Emadd2

*w/o vol. pedal

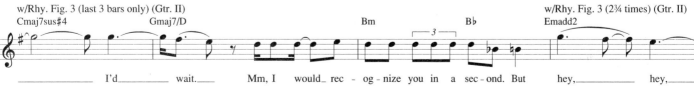

w/Rhy. Fig. 3 (last 3 bars only) (Gtr. II)   w/Rhy. Fig. 3 (2¾ times) (Gtr. II)
Cmaj7sus#4   Gmaj7/D   Bm   B♭   Emadd2

_____ I'd_____ wait._____ Mm, I would_ rec-og-nize you in a sec-ond. But   hey,_____ hey,_____

122

GRANNY

Words and Music by
David J. Matthews

* Play all gtr. parts w/slight variations ad lib when repeated or recalled (throughout).
** Acous.

* Drop-D tuning: ⑥ = D

1st, 2nd Verses
w/Rhy. Fig. 1 (3½ times)

1. Hel - lo,_____ how are___ you do - ing_____ to - day?___ I hope_
2. *See additional lyrics*

* Composite arrangement; 6th & 5th stgs. played by Gtr. II only.

Additional Lyrics

2. Well, here we are, all of us stand around.
   We're leaning heavy on each other.
   Always wondering what is it lies behind
   The worried eyes of one another.

2nd Pre-chorus
I believe it's love that's hiding there out in the shadows, in the darkness.
Maybe we shed a little light and it will shine.
Oh, love, when I approach, my tears, they fall like rain 'cause you know. . .
Baby, my heart into a thousand pieces dashed. *(To Chorus)*

3rd Pre-chorus
I say it's love, so share it out. Share it fair but share it liberal.
Maybe I think it's a better world that it could build up.
But, love, when I approach, the tears, they fall like rain, you tell me. . .
Baby, your heart into a thousand pieces dashed. *(To Chorus)*

• Tablature Explanation/Notation Legend •

TABLATURE: A six-line staff that graphically represents the guitar fingerboard. By placing a number on the appropriate line, the string and the fret of any note can be indicated. For example:

```
1st string - High E ─────────────────────────────────────── 0 ───
2nd string - B     ─────────────────────── 10 ────────────── 0 ───
3rd string - G     ─────────────────────── 9 ─────────────── 1 ───
4th string - D     ──────────────────────────────────────── 2 ───
5th string - A     ───── 3 ───────────────────────────────── 2 ───
6th string - Low E ──────────────────────────────────────── 0 ───
```

5th string, 3rd fret   2nd string, 10th fret   an open E chord
                              and 3rd string, 9th fret
                              played together

Definitions for Special Guitar Notation

BEND: Strike the note and bend up a half step (one fret).

BEND: Strike the note and bend up a whole step (two frets).

BEND AND RELEASE: Strike the note and bend up a half (or whole) step, then release the bend back to the original note. All three notes are tied; only the first note is struck.

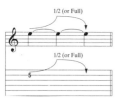

PRE-BEND: Bend the note up a half (or whole) step, then strike it.

PRE-BEND AND RELEASE: Bend the note up a half (or whole) step, strike it and release the bend back to the original note.

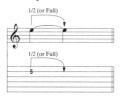

UNISON BEND: Strike the two notes simultaneously and bend the lower note to the pitch of the higher.

VIBRATO: Vibrate the note by rapidly bending and releasing the string with a left-hand finger.

WIDE OR EXAGGERATED VIBRATO: Vibrate the pitch to a greater degree with a left-hand finger or the tremolo bar.

SLIDE: Strike the first note and then with the same left-hand finger move up the string to the second note. The second note is not struck.

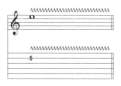

SLIDE: Same as above, except the second note is struck.

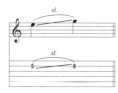

SLIDE: Slide up to the note indicated from a few frets below.

HAMMER-ON: Strike the first (lower) note, then sound the higher note with another finger by fretting it without picking.

PULL-OFF: Place both fingers on the notes to be sounded. Strike the first (higher) note, then sound the lower note by pulling the finger off the higher note while keeping the lower note fretted.

TRILL: Very rapidly alternate between the note indicated and the small note shown in parentheses by hammering on and pulling off.

TAPPING: Hammer ("tap") the fret indicated with the right-hand index or middle finger and pull off to the note fretted by the left hand.

NATURAL HARMONIC: With a left-hand finger, lightly touch the string over the fret indicated, then strike it. A chime-like sound is produced.

ARTIFICIAL HARMONIC: Fret the note normally and sound the harmonic by adding the right-hand thumb edge or index finger tip to the normal pick attack.

A.H. pitch: E

TREMOLO BAR: Drop the note by the number of steps indicated, then return to original pitch.

PALM MUTE: With the right hand, partially mute the note by lightly touching the string just before the bridge.

MUFFLED STRINGS: Lay the left hand across the strings without depressing them to the fretboard; strike the strings with the right hand, producing a percussive sound.

PICK SLIDE: Rub the pick edge down the length of the string to produce a scratchy sound.

pick slide

TREMOLO PICKING: Pick the note as rapidly and continuously as possible

trem. pick

RHYTHM SLASHES: Strum chords in rhythm indicated. Use chord voicings found in the fingering diagrams at the top of the first page of the transcription.

Am   D

SINGLE-NOTE RHYTHM SLASHES: The circled number above the note name indicates which string to play. When successive notes are played on the same string, only the fret numbers are given.

⑤ 3fr.   2fr. open ⑥ 3fr.
C   B   A   G